TIMESAVER PHRASAL VERBS AND IDIOMS

Teacher's reference key

A small clock on each page tells you approximately how long each activity should take.

Contents

● Students with one or more years of English
●● Students with two or more years of English
●●● Students with three or more years of English

Page	Title	Activity	Language	Level
35	**Domino Game with *turn***	Matching game	Phrasal verbs with *turn*	●●
36 & 37	**What's the Difference?**	Finding the differences between two pictures	Idioms	●●
38	**What's the Punch-line?**	Matching definitions and punch-lines	Phrasal verbs	●●
39	**Body Language**	Choosing the correct definition	Idioms connected with the body	●●
40 & 41	**Board Game 2**	Group board game	Phrasal verbs and idioms	●●
42	**Animal Behaviour**	Picture gap-fill	Idioms connected with animals	●●
43	**Dinner Time**	Picture gap-fill	Idioms connected with food and drink	●●
44	**Fact or Fiction?**	True or false quiz	Phrasal verbs and compound nouns	●●●
45	**The Criminal Quiz**	Matching pictures to questions	Phrasal verbs	●●●
46 & 47	**True Stories?**	True or false quiz	Phrasal verbs	●●●
48 & 49	**The Perfect Job**	Personality questionnaire	Idioms	●●●
50 & 51	**Super Grid: *up***	Gap-fill grid	Phrasal verbs with 'up'	●●●
52, 53 & 54	**Super Grid: *down* & Do-it-yourself Grid**	Gap-fill grid, making sentences with phrasal verbs	Phrasal verbs with 'down'	●●●
55	**Idiom Crossword**	Crossword	Idioms connected to geography and the weather	●●●
56 & 57	**Clowns International**	Gap-fill, role play	Phrasal verbs	●●●
58, 59 & 60	**Pocahontas**	Gap-fill, discussions	Phrasal verbs with 'set' and general phrasal verbs	●●●
61	**Colour Codes**	Gap-fill maze	Idioms with colours	●●●
62 & 63	**Relationship Questionnaire**	Personality quiz	Idioms	●●●
64	**Mind Matching 2**	Team game: completing sentences	Phrasal verbs and idioms	●●●
65	**Around the House**	Picture gap-fill	Idioms connected to the house	●●●
66, 67, 68 & 69	**War of the Roses**	Paired gap-fill, re-ordering paragraphs	Idioms and phrasal verbs	●●●
70 & 71	**A Pop Star's Diary**	Word circle gap-fill	Idioms for comparison: *as .... as*	●●●
72 & 73	**Board Game 3**	Group board game	Phrasal verbs and idioms	●●●
74 & 75	**Board Game template**	'Board' needed for board games 1, 2 and 3.		

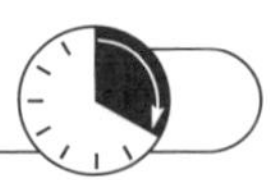

Christmas List

It is the 24th December. This morning, Father Christmas made a list of all the things he had to do today before his busy night. Put a ✔ under *Yes* for the things he has done and a ✔ under *No* for the things he hasn't done.

Things To Do!	Yes	No
1 Bring the sledge in from the garage	☐ w	☐ l
2 Let the reindeer out	☐ b	☐ a
3 Pick the elves up from the factory	☐ k	☐ a
4 Put the decorations up	☐ i	☐ e
5 Don't burn the mince pies! turn the oven off at 3.00	☐ t	☐ u
6 Wash up	☐ p	☐ y
7 Pick red suit up from the dry cleaner's	☐ s	☐ e
8 Send Christmas cards off	☐ v	☐ a
9 Put up the Christmas tree	☐ e	☐ n
10 Wrap the presents up	☐ s	☐ t
11 Take the rubbish out	☐ w	☐ a

Now, write the letters next to your answers in the little boy's speech bubble. If your answers are correct, you will find out what he is saying to Father Christmas.

__ __ __ __
1 2 3 4

__ __
5 6

__ __ __ __ __ !
7 8 9 10 11

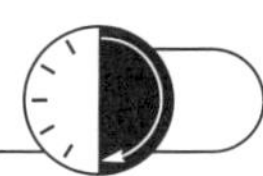

Doctor, Doctor

Each joke is missing one phrasal verb.
Write the correct phrasal verbs from the box below in the correct jokes.

Phrasal Verbs
come back • stick out • lie down • give up
going on • add up • come across • lift up
turn up • work out • go out

1 Patient: Doctor, doctor, I think I'm a dog

Doctor: ________ on the sofa and tell me about it.

Patient: ....

2 Patient: Doctor, doctor, I'm not feeling well.

Doctor: Go to the window and ________ your tongue.

Patient: Will that help you to ________ what's wrong with me?

Doctor: ....

3 Patient: Doctor, doctor, every time I ________ anywhere people ignore me.

Doctor: ....

4 Patient: Doctor, doctor, every time I ________ my left arm I get a pain.

Doctor: ....

5 Patient: Doctor, doctor, I keep stealing things from shops.

Doctor: Take this big strong bag with you next time you ________ .

Patient: Will that help me to ________ stealing?

Doctor: ....

6 Patient: Doctor, doctor, you gave me some pills to make me stronger.

Doctor: So, why have you ________ ? Didn't the pills work?

Patient: ....

7 Patient: Doctor, doctor, I have a terrible memory.

Doctor: How long has this been ________ ?

Patient: ....

8 Patient: Doctor, doctor, I can't ________

Doctor: When did this problem start?

Patient: ....

9 Patient: Doctor, doctor, I think I'm a telephone.

Doctor: How strange, I've never ________ this before. Are you married?

Patient: ....

Read the jokes again. Can you find the correct punchline for each joke?

Punchlines

a) *Not at all, but could you get me a colour television next time you go shopping?*

b) *No, not at all, I just don't like the man who lives across the road.*

c) *Then don't do it.*

d) *I'm sorry I can't do that, I'm not allowed on the furniture.*

e) *I don't know. I couldn't get the top off the bottle.*

f) *38th March*

g) *How long has what been going on?*

h) *Next, please.*

i) *No, but I'm engaged.*

The Elephant Joke

Complete the phrasal verbs, using the prepositions above.

An elephant walks 1 .... a restaurant, sits 2 .... at a table near the window and says to the waiter, "Good morning, could I have a cup of coffee, please?"

The waiter is amazed. "What's wrong?" the elephant asks, "You look like you've seen a ghost".

"I'm sorry. I've never heard an elephant talking before, and you speak perfect English."

"I don't know why you're surprised" the elephant says, "I'm Indian, I grew 3 .... in Bombay, and a lot of people speak English there. I can speak other languages, too. I'm fluent in French and Japanese and I can get 4 .... in Spanish and Danish. Anyway, can I have my coffee, now?"

"I'm afraid we've run 5 .... of coffee, Sir, but how about a nice cup of tea?"

"Tea?" says the elephant "Yes, that'll be fine."

So the waiter goes into the kitchen and tells the manager that there is an Indian elephant sitting by the window, who wants a cup of tea.

"OK," says the manager, "We'd better give him some tea, then."

The waiter goes 6 .... to the elephant and says, "Here's your tea, Sir, and here's your bill for £3.50."

The elephant says "Thank you," picks up the cup with his trunk, and starts drinking. But a few moments later, the elephant throws the cup and the tray 7 .... the floor and starts shouting.

The waiter is terrified, and says, "What's wrong, Sir?"

"It's this tea," the elephant says, "you put milk in it. Don't you know ANYTHING about elephants? We NEVER put milk in our tea!"

"I'm really sorry," the waiter says, "I didn't realise. It's just that we don't come 8 .... many elephants in this part of the world."

"That's not surprising," the elephant says, "£3.50 for a cup of tea is much too expensive!"

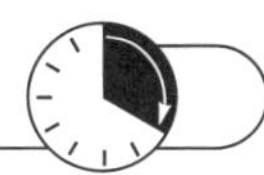

Picture Connections

Match A and B to make C. Connect a picture from the first column with a picture from the second column to make a compound noun which you find in the third column. For example, sea + horse = seahorse. Write the compound noun next to the picture in the third column.

	A	B	C	
1				....
2				....
3				....
4				....
5				....
6				*seahorse*
7				....
8				....
9				....

Who's Who?

1. Match the sentence halves to make descriptions of the people in the picture.
2. Write the names of the people next to them in the picture.

1 Patricia hasn't eaten since breakfast.
2 Jane's just got engaged.
3 Mr Johnson lives next door. He doesn't like parties.
4 Henry is going bald.
5 Mark wants to be a footballer.
6 Greg tripped over the dog and fell down the stairs.
7 Karen's very rich.
8 Albert's not very friendly.
9 Olga is terrible at dancing.
10 Victoria keeps falling asleep.
11 Trevor isn't very well at the moment.

a) He's a cold fish.
b) He's following in his father's footsteps.
c) She's so hungry she could eat a horse.
d) He's under the weather.
e) He's a bit thin on top.
f) The noise is driving him up the wall.
g) She's rolling in it.
h) She's over the moon.
i) She's got two left feet.
j) He's been in the wars.
k) She's been burning the candle at both ends.

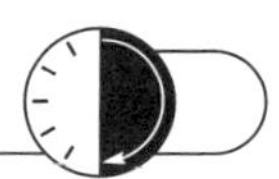

Mind Matching 1

Instructions for the teacher

1 Photocopy the chart below so that there is one for each person in the class.

2 Divide the class into two teams. Each team should nominate someone from their group to be the 'player'. The two players must go to the front of the class, so that they are facing their teams.

3 Give one of the photocopied charts to everyone, including the two players at the front of the class. Ask everyone to complete the first three squares on their chart. The students must not talk to each other or show anyone what they have written.

4 When everyone has finished writing, read out the first question. The two players should then read out their answers to the first question.

5 Everyone from both teams must then read out their answer to the first question. Teams score one point for each person who has the same answer as their team player. (To prevent cheating, move around the class and check what the students have written on their charts.)

6 Read out the second question and repeat the process. When you have heard all of the answers for the first three questions, ask the students to write down their answers to the next three, and continue the game. The team with the most points wins.

Alternative

For a smaller class, play as one team, with one player. Each person scores one point for every answer that matches the player's answer. The winner is the student with the most points at the end of the game.

Write down...

1 ...something that you <u>put up</u> when it's raining.	**2** ...something that you <u>turn off</u> before you leave the house.	**3** ...something that you <u>put on</u> before you go to bed.
4 ...the name of a famous person that you <u>look up to</u>.	**5** ...an occasion that you <u>dress up for</u>.	**6** ...a situation in which you shout <u>"Look out!"</u>
7 ...a situation in which you get <u>butterflies in your stomach</u>.	**8** ...something that's <u>not your cup of tea</u>.	**9** ...something you do <u>once in a blue moon</u>.
10 ...a good way to <u>break the ice</u>.	**11** ...a situation in which people tell a <u>white lie</u>.	**12** ... someone who spends money like it's <u>going out of fashion</u>.

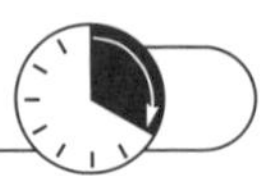

All at Sea

Student A

**Find the differences between your picture and your partner's picture.
Fill the gaps in each sentence to find clues.**

1 Have you seen Jean Marc's new girlfriend? She's as pretty as a ....

2 I don't like tennis. It's just not my ....

3 What's your new teacher called? Michael Jones, hmm… that name rings a ....

4 I couldn't answer the first question, but the rest of the test was plain ....ing.

5 My brother's a footballer. He's 18 and he's just been signed up by Barcelona.
He's got the world at his ....

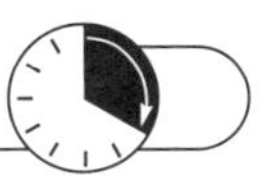

All at Sea

Student B

Find the differences between your picture and your partner's picture. Fill the gaps in each sentence to find clues.

1 My brother and sister don't get on. They don't see eye to ....

2 Is it your first day here? Don't worry, I'll show you the ....

3 The weather is awful. It's raining cats and ....

4 Lucy will be really angry when she finds out you copied her homework. I wouldn't like to be in your .... when she finds out what happened.

5 I know you're sad because you've broken up with your boyfriend, but remember, there are plenty more .... in the sea.

Signs

Use the phrasal verbs below to complete the signs.
Then match the signs and the places you would find them.

take away • pick up • keep off • switch off • try on • check in
give up • check out • closing down • slow down

1

Please ....
your mobile phone
before the film begins!

2

Please ....
this seat if an elderly person
needs it!

3

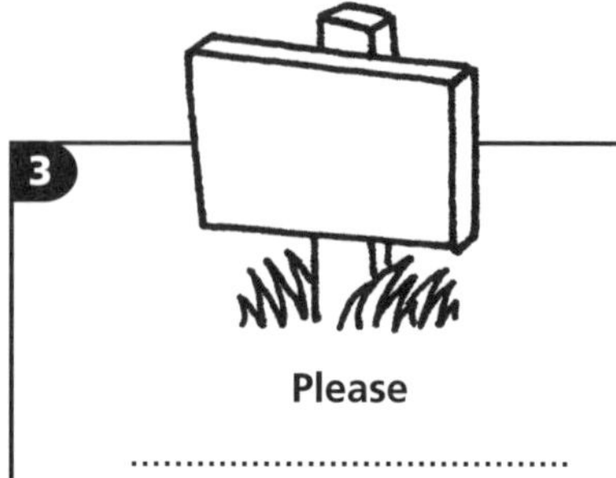

Please
....
the grass!

4

.... !
Road Works
ahead!

5

Presto Prints
Get your photos in an hour.
Drop your film off at 4.
....
your pictures at 5!

6

Presto Pizzas
The best in town. Eat in or
....

7

If you want to
.... clothes,
please use the changing rooms
on the first floor.

8

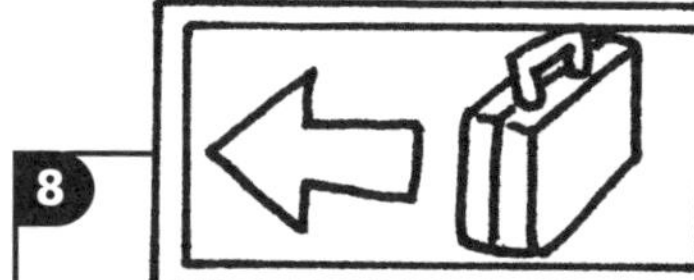

Please ....
an hour before your
plane takes off.

9

Please ....
before midday.

10

.... sale!
Last few days...
everything must go.

Places

a) restaurant	☐	**f)** road	☐
b) cinema	☐	**g)** photography shop	☐
c) clothes shop	☐	**h)** hotel	☐
d) bus	☐	**i)** shop window	☐
e) airport	☐	**j)** park	☐

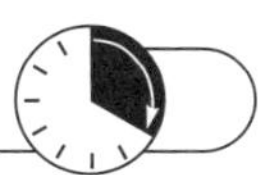

Surfing the Web

Find the eight missing words in the grid. Then put the captions into the correct order.

W	E	P	A	S	S	W	O	R	D
H	F	L	L	W	H	R	O	Z	M
C	Z	U	C	I	U	J	U	F	P
L	O	G	F	T	T	Y	P	E	K
I	P	Y	S	C	R	O	L	L	F
C	B	D	L	H	V	A	Z	D	W
K	P	R	I	N	T	O	R	P	E

a) T................. in the website address. ☐

b) Log off, s.................. down the computer and switch it off. ☐

c) S................. the computer on. ☐

d) S................. down the page. ☐

e) L................. on, using your password. ☐

f) P................. out the information you want. ☐

g) C................. on the Internet symbol. ☐

i) P................. the computer in. ☐

1 ☐

2 ☐

ON/OFF

3 ☐

PLEASE ENTER YOUR PASSWORD

****

4 ☐

INTERNET

5 ☐

WWW.SITE@

6 ☐

7 ☐

8 ☐

DO YOU WANT TO LOG OFF?

YES NO

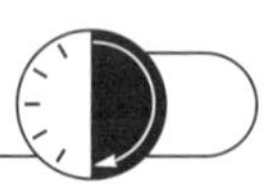

Carla goes on Holiday

Carla goes on Holiday

Instructions for the teacher
This game should be played in small groups. Photocopy the 28 pictures from the opposite page and the 28 sentences cards below, so that there is one set of pictures and sentences for each group. Before you hand out the cards, make sure that each set has been shuffled. The students must work together to put the pictures in the correct sequence and then put the correct sentence card with each picture.

Follow up
Take away the sentences, leaving just the cartoon sequence. The students have to remember the phrasal verbs that go with each picture. (For more advanced groups, ask the students to repeat whole sentences.) One student from each group is allowed to look at the sentences. He / she can tell the other students whether their guesses are correct or incorrect, but must not give clues. The winning group is the first to repeat the story (or phrasal verb sequence) correctly without the sentence cards.

1 At 5.30, the alarm goes off in Carla's bedroom.	She wakes up.	She turns off the alarm.	She gets up.
She puts on her dressing gown.	She makes breakfast, but the milk boils over.	She washes up.	She picks up her suitcase.
She waits for a bus.	She gets to the airport.	She checks in.	The security staff put her bag through the x-ray machine.
She goes through passport control.	She sits down in the departure lounge.	She gets on the plane.	She looks for her seat.
She puts her bag into the locker.	She puts on her seatbelt.	The plane takes off.	The stewardess comes round with drinks.
Carla puts on headphones and watches a film.	The stewardess comes through the plane collecting the headphones.	The plane lands and Carla takes off her seatbelt.	She takes her bag out of the locker.
She picks up her suitcase from the carousel.	She gets on the hotel bus.	She fills in the registration form at the hotel.	**28** She lets herself into room 109, falls onto the bed, stretches out and dozes off.

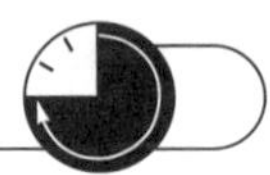

Board Game 1

Instructions for the teacher
Divide the class into groups of four. Each group will need:
- one copy of the board on pages 74 & 75
- one set of idiom cards
- one set of phrasal verb cards
- a die
- a counter for each player

Rules of the game
Player 1 must role the die and move his / her counter the corresponding number of spaces along the board. If the space that they land on has instructions, such as 'Go forward 3' they must do as the instructions say. If they land on a square that says 'phrasal verbs' or 'idioms', another player must pick up a card from the appropriate pile and read out the question on it. If player 1 gives the correct answer, they may role the die again and have another go. If player 1 gives the wrong answer, play passes to the next person. The winner is the first person to get around the board, from beginning to end.

Idioms

If a person has green fingers what are they good at?
a) knitting
b) gardening
c) cooking
Answer: gardening

What does it mean if something is a piece of cake?
a) it's delicious
b) it smells nice
c) it's easy
Answer: It's easy

If you're a cold fish, what are you?
a) unhealthy
b) unfriendly
c) unmarried
Answer: unfriendly

What does it mean if you've got a lot on your plate?
a) you're hungry
b) you're lazy
c) you're busy
Answer: You're busy

If you're over the moon, how do you feel?
a) happy
b) full of energy
c) stupid
Answer: happy

If I give you a hand, what do I do?
a) hit you
b) help you
c) marry you
Answer: I help you

If you've got a sweet tooth, what kind of things do you like to eat?
a) chicken and chips
b) carrots and potatoes
c) cakes and chocolates
Answer: cakes and chocolates

If you are two-faced, what are you?
a) beautiful
b) dishonest
c) greedy
Answer: dishonest

What does it mean if you get a letter out of the blue?
a) the letter makes you sad
b) the letter was from a stranger
c) you were not expecting the letter
Answer: You were not expecting the letter

What does it mean if you're all at sea?
a) you are travelling
b) you are dreaming
c) things are going badly
Answer: Things are going badly

If someone says, "Football's not my cup of tea," what do they mean?
a) they don't like football
b) they love football
c) they like football, but they prefer tea
Answer: They don't like football

What does it mean if you have a heart of gold?
a) you are very rich
b) you are in love
c) you are very kind
Answer: You are very kind

If your computer's a bit of a white elephant, what is it like?
a) it's useless
b) it's unusual
c) it's from a hot country
Answer: It's useless

If you're off colour, how are you feeling?
a) ill
b) tired
c) bored
Answer: ill

If something is the cat's whiskers, what's it like?
a) it's awful
b) it's great
c) it's tiny
Answer: It's great

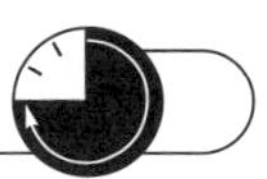

Board Game 1

Phrasal Verbs

If your computer has broken down, what has happened?

a) It has stopped working
b) It has started working
c) You have turned it off

Answer: It has stopped working

If someone gives up cigarettes, what do they do?

a) They start smoking
b) They stop smoking
c) They give cigarettes to their friends

Answer: They stop smoking

If a shop puts up the price of something, what happens?

a) It gets cheaper
b) It gets more expensive
c) You don't have to pay for it

Answer: It gets more expensive

Where do you have to check in?

a) at a restaurant
b) at a library
c) at an airport

Answer: at an airport

Why would you take something back to a shop?

a) It doesn't work
b) You want to pay for it
c) You like it

Answer: It doesn't work

If you put your feet up what are you doing?

a) cycling
b) running
c) resting

Answer: resting

What does it mean if the milk has gone off?

a) There is no milk left
b) The milk isn't fresh
c) Somebody has spilt the milk

Answer: The milk isn't fresh

What takes off from a runway?

a) a train
b) a plane
c) a car

Answer: a plane

What pulls out of a station?

a) a train
b) a plane
c) a car

Answer: a train

Who looks after animals?

a) a ticket inspector
b) a builder
c) a zookeeper

Answer: a zookeeper

If I tell you off, what does it mean?

a) I'm telling you something
b) I'm angry with you
c) I'm pleased with you

Answer: I'm angry with you

What does it mean if I carry on with something?

a) I continue to do something
b) I stop doing something
c) I start doing something

Answer: I continue to do something

Who looks after children when their parents are out?

a) a zookeeper
b) a traffic warden
c) a babysitter

Answer: a babysitter

What does the expression 'hang on' mean?

a) Wait a moment!
b) Come here!
c) Go away!

Answer: Wait a moment!

What could you try on in a shop?

a) a kettle
b) a computer
c) a pair of trousers

Answer: a pair of trousers

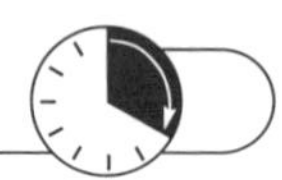

Fruit Salad!

Put a word in the gap that can go after the word on the left and before the word on the right to make the things shown in the two pictures. For example...

 fruit s a l a d dressing 

1   fountain ___ ___ ___ knife

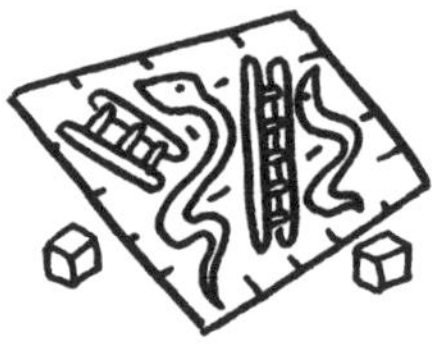

2 key ___ ___ ___ ___ ___ ___ game

3 sign ___ ___ ___ ___ office

4 light ___ ___ ___ ___ ___ work

5 day ___ ___ ___ ___ ___ fast

6 

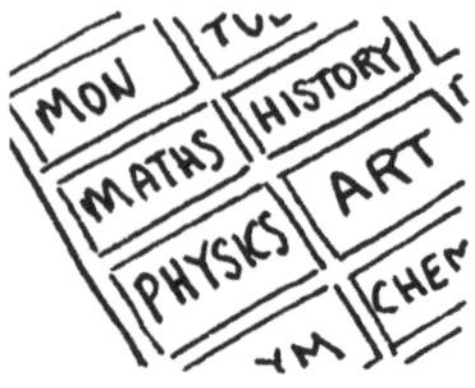

time ___ ___ ___ ___ ___ tennis

7 tin ___ ___ ___ opener

8 river ___ ___ ___ ___ robber

9 girl ___ ___ ___ ___ ___ book

10 life ___ ___ ___ ___ ___ ___ potato

11  

car ___ ___ ___ ___ ___ clock

12  

traffic ___ ___ ___ doughnut

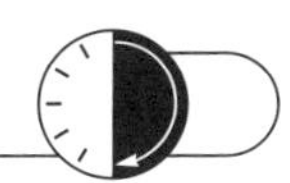

Sports Quiz

Complete the sentences with the prepositions in the box, then check your answers by using the same prepositions to make words at the bottom of the page.

out ~ out ~ out ~ out ~ off ~ off ~ off ~ up ~ up ~ up ~ up ~ in ~ on ~ on

1 A football match starts with a kick-________ .

8 If the referee shows you a red card, you are sent ________ .

2 A basketball game begins with a throw-________ .

9 In basketball and American football, you can stop the match for a time-________ .

3 Many people go to the gym to work ________ .

10 Before exercising you should always warm ________ with some stretching exercises.

4 In football, if the ball goes out of play you can have a goalkick, a corner or a throw-________ .

11 A supporter is someone who cheers his or her team ________ .

5 Before a tennis match, the players have a knock-________ .

12 Professional sports players are dedicated to working ________ their game.

6 A boxer can win a fight with a knock-________ .

13 It's a good idea to take ________ a sport if you want to get fit.

7 In the football World Cup, some matches are decided by a penalty shoot-________ .

14 There is always the danger that a tennis match will be rained ________ at Wimbledon.

Now use the 14 prepositions to complete these words and to check your answers.

1 a c______ee pot

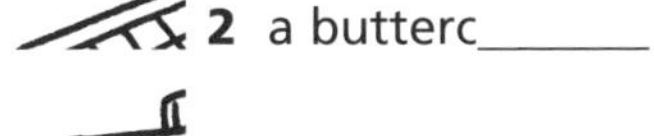

2 a butterc______

3 inside, ______side

4 a safety p______

5 an eggc______

6 the m______h of a river

7 east, west, north, s______h

8 a t______fe apple

9 a roundab______

10 a c______board

11 bac______

12 ______ion

13 p______py

14 ______ice building

The Traveller

**Look at the pictures below. What do the people look like?
How long do you think they have been travelling?
What places do you think they have travelled to?
What do you think their lives are like?**

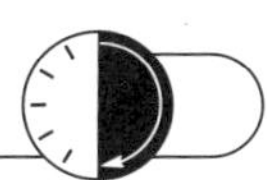

The Traveller

Student A

Imagine you are one of the people in the pictures. You meet Student B for the first time. He / she is very interested in your life and asks you lots of questions. You are happy to talk about your life. Before you start, think of the following:

- your childhood / family background
- how you ended up travelling
- whether you enjoy your life or not
- what kind of person you are
- your daily life
- the people you've met and experiences you've had

Student B

Imagine you meet one of the people in the pictures (Student A). You are very interested in the kind of life he / she has led. You have lots of questions to ask him / her. Read through the questions and make sure you understand them fully.

1 Where do you come from?

2 Where did you grow up?

3 How did you end up here?

4 Did you fall out with your family?

5 What have you found out about yourself by living on the road?

6 If I wanted to live the same life as you, would you try and put me off?

7 Do you come across strange people on the road?

8 Do you find it difficult to get on with other people? Do you find it difficult to fit in?

9 How do you get by?

10 What do people make of you? Do they look down on you?

11 What sort of things do you have to do without?

12 Has anyone ever put you up in their home for a night?

13 What are the good things about living on the road? And what are the drawbacks?

14 Do you feel free because there's nobody to tell you off or order you about, or do you feel cut off from society in some way?

15 Can you take me through a typical day? How do you spend your time?

Picture Interviews

Student A

Your partner will ask you some questions. Use the pictures below to answer them. Then ask your questions and write down the answers that your partner gives you.

1 Why have they called off the football match?
a) It's been snowing heavily.
b) It's been raining heavily.

2 Why is Kerry putting by £5 a week?
a) She is saving up to buy a motorbike.
b) She is saving up to buy a bicycle.

3 Why is the cat putting on weight?
a) She's eating a lot of sausages.
b) She's eating a lot of bananas.

4 Why is Mr Robson putting the kettle on?
a) He wants to make a hot water bottle.
b) He wants to make some tea for his friends.

5 What has put Michael off his soup?
a) He has found a hair in it.
b) He has found a hare in it.

6 What has put the traffic warden out?
a) A car has just driven through a puddle and splashed her.
b) It's so hot that she can't concentrate on her work.

Now together, think of:
- another reason why you'd call off a football match
- something that might make you put on weight
- something else that could put you off your food
- something that would really put you out

Picture Interviews

Student B

Ask your questions and write down the answers that your partner gives you. Then use the pictures below to answer your partner's questions.

1 Why can't the helicopter take off?
a) The weather is really bad.
b) The helicopter isn't ready yet.

2 Who does Anka take after?
a) Her mother.
b) Her father.

3 Yoko bought a jacket without trying it on first. Why should she now take it back to the shop?
a) It's much too big for her.
b) The sleeves are much too short.

4 Why did Lee and George take to each other straight away?
a) They have a common interest.
b) They have nothing in common.

5 Why has Harry taken up karate?
a) To stop bullies picking on him.
b) To get out of having to tidy up his bedroom.

6 Who has been taken in by the conman?
a) The old man.
b) The young woman.

Now together, think of:
- another reason why a helicopter might not take off
- something else you might take back to a shop
- something else you can take up
- a time when you were taken in by someone

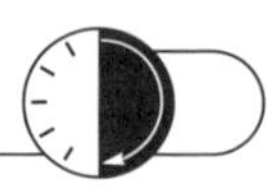

The Ladder

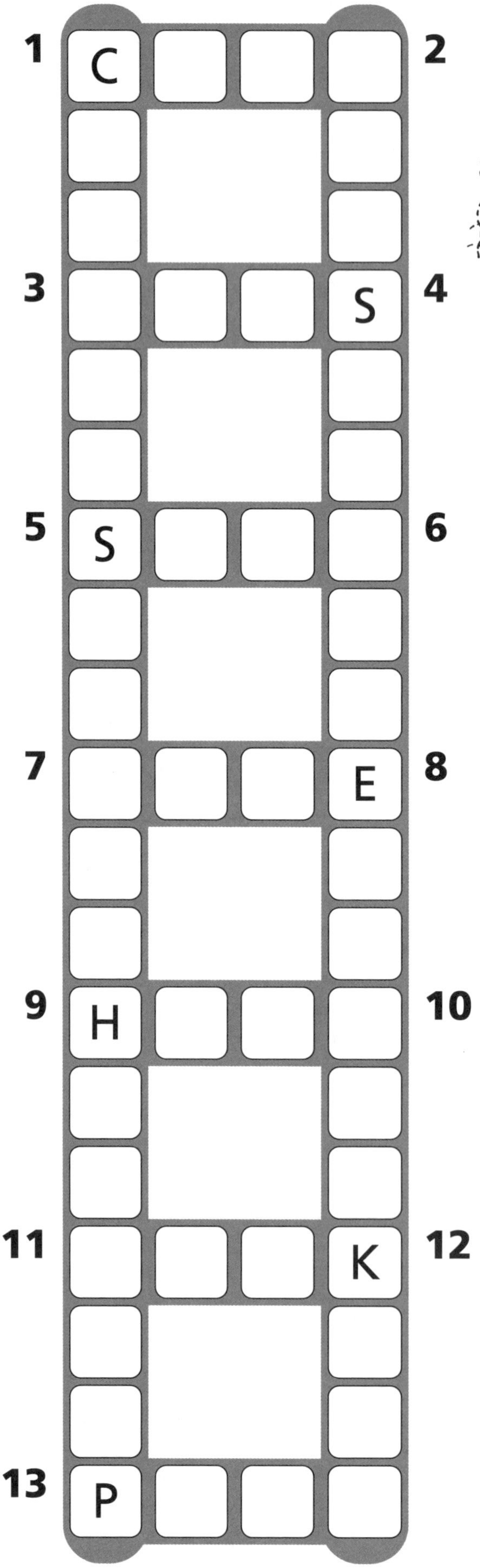

1	C				2
3				S	4
5	S				6
7				E	8
9	H				10
11				K	12
13	P				

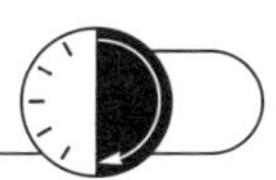

The Ladder

Complete the Ladder Crossword with the words missing from the punch-lines below.

Clues

1 across
Why did Marvo the Sword swallower lose his job?
Because he was always biting off more than he could …………………… .

1 down
Why did the crossword compiler lose her job?
Because she didn't have a …………………… .

2 down
Why do jelly makers do exactly the same thing every day?
Because they're very set in their …………………… .

3 across
Why did the bridge builder lose her job?
Because she couldn't make …………………… meet.

3 down
Why did the dishonest shepherd lose his job?
Because he was always trying to pull the wool over people's …………………… .

4 down
Why did the yoghurt stop dating the lemon?
Because their relationship turned …………………… .

5 across
Why do forks hate spoons?
Because spoons like to …………………… up trouble.

5 down
Cowboy 1: Why did you buy those horrible boots?
Cowboy 2: There was a sale in the shoe shop and I bought them the …………………… of the moment.

6 down
Why is tightrope walking a popular job?
Because it's money for old …………………… .

7 across
Why should you never trust a bus driver?
Because he'll take you for a …………………… .

7 down
Why are people with money smelly?
Because they're stinking …………………… .

8 down
Why are swimmers always naive?
Because they're wet behind the …………………… .

9 across
Why is the hammer the most intelligent tool of all?
Because it always …………………… the nail on the head.

9 down
Why did the acrobats get married?
Because they were …………………… over heels in love.

10 down
Why does Santa Claus go to the job centre every January?
Because he always gets the …………………… at Christmas.

11 across
Did he warn you that he was going to turn off the light?
No I was left in the …………………… about it.

11 down
Was the lifeguard's first day at work easy?
Not at all, they threw him in at the …………………… end.

12 down
Why did he throw his watch off a cliff?
Because he was trying to …………………… time.

13 across
How did you get a job as a puppeteer?
I asked a friend to …………………… a few strings for me.

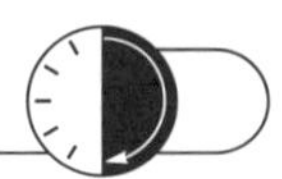

Act It Out

Instructions for the teacher
Photocopy the illustrated list of phrasal verbs and go through them with their meanings with the students. The students should keep their lists to refer to during the game.

Divide the class into small groups. Give each group a pile of mime cards which they must place face down. The students must take it in turns to pick up a card and mime the situation on it. Before the students begin their mimes, they must read out the first sentence on the card, which tells the rest of the group what information they are looking for, e.g. *You are looking for a place and a phrasal verb.* The others must guess what is being mimed. This version of the game is just for fun and there is no scoring involved.

Alternative
Divide the class into two teams. Ask a student from Team A to come to the front, pick up a card and mime the situation. Students from both teams can try to guess what is being mimed. The first student to guess correctly scores a point for their team. A student from Team B must then do a mime. The game continues until all of the cards have been used.

Note: Some of the mimes are for two people. When two people are needed, it is indicated on the card.

You are looking for a place and a phrasal verb.

Mime
You are standing at a bus stop, waiting for a bus.

You are looking for a place and a phrasal verb.

Mime
You are checking in at an airport.

You are looking for a place and two phrasal verbs.

Mime
You are at a restaurant. You sit down and look at the menu.

You are looking for a place and two phrasal verbs.

Mime
You are in bed. You wake up and turn off the alarm clock.

You are looking for a kind of food and a phrasal verb.

Mime
You blow out the candles on your birthday cake.

This mime is for two people.
You are looking for a place and two phrasal verbs

Mime
You are working on the checkout of a supermarket. The bar code scanner breaks down. The customer get really angry, you try to get him / her to calm down.

This mime is for two people.
You are looking for a place and two phrasal verbs.

Mime
You go into a café and see a friend sitting at one of the tables. He / she looks sad. Go over to him / her and try to cheer them up.

You are looking for an object and two phrasal verbs.

Mime
You are reading a newspaper when you see a picture of your favourite film star. Cut the picture out and put it up on your wall.

You are looking for 2 objects and two phrasal verbs

Mime
You are on a park bench. The weather changes and it gets very cold, and then it starts to rain. Do up your coat and put up your umbrella.

You are looking for a place and two phrasal verbs.

Mime
You are at a petrol station. You fill up your car but then drive off without paying.

This is a mime for two people.
You are looking for a place and one phrasal verb

Mime
You are at in a clothes shop and you bump into an old friend.

This is a mime for two people.
You are looking for a place and two phrasal verbs.

Mime
You are at a train station, seeing your friend off. You chat for a while then the train pulls out of the station and you wave.

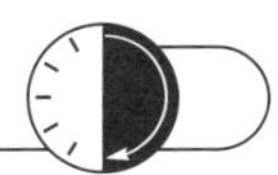

Act It Out

Phrasal Verbs

cut out

do up

cheer up

wait for

put up

wake up

bump into

see (someone) off

go over

check in

look at

blow out

fill up

pull out of

drive off

turn off

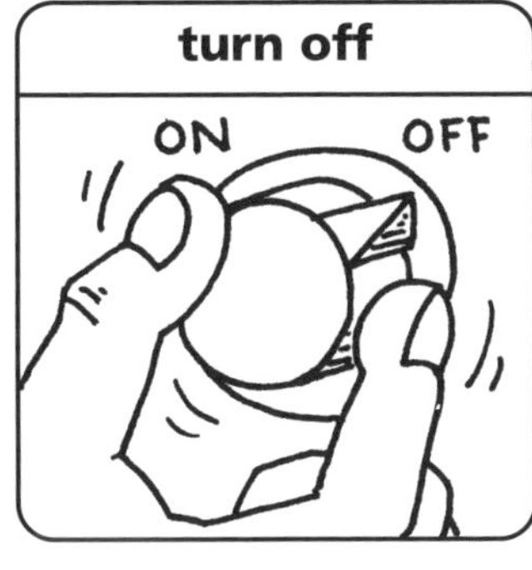

calm down

break down

sit down

Hotel Magnifico

Student A

Mona Lott didn't enjoy her holiday at the Hotel Magnifico, so after the holiday she wrote a letter to the travel agent with a list of her complaints. Use these phrasal verbs with *run* to complete her letter.

through • over • out of • away • after • up • into • down

Dear Sir,

I am writing to complain about my recent holiday at the Hotel Magnifico. Let me just run (1) .... some of the main problems we had.

Firstly, your brochure claimed that the local people were very friendly and welcoming. However, on our arrival at the airport, we were attacked by a strange man who ran into my husband with a baggage trolley causing him a serious injury. We still don't know the cost of the medical bills we have run (2) .... because of this incident. The attacker also took our suitcase, but luckily I managed to run (3) .... him and get our bag back.

As for the location of the hotel, you promised us that it was located in a pleasant neighbourhood. However, just 200 metres away, there were dozens of old buildings that were really run (4) .... Some of the buildings didn't even have a roof on them!

The brochure claimed that the town was very safe but when I drove down to the beach there were several cars travelling on the wrong side of the road and I had to swerve to avoid them. On one occasion I nearly ran (5) .... a pedestrian who crossed the road without looking in my direction at all.

I'm afraid I ran (6) .... a few problems with the hotel staff too. They didn't speak English so I tried to speak their language but when I told them that I was sick of the food in the restaurant, they all just ran (7) ....

On a happier note, we thought it was a nice touch leaving those bowls of complimentary salad in our room. But why was the salad all red and blue? Had you run (8) .... green salad like lettuce and cucumber?

Yours faithfully

Mona Lott

Now work in pairs. Match the phrasal verbs and their definitions.

1 run through
2 run over
3 run out of
4 run away
5 run after
6 run up (a bill)
7 run down
8 run into (a problem)

a) chase, follow
b) leave quickly
c) hit someone with a vehicle
d) allow to deteriorate, criticise
e) use something up, have none left
f) spend a lot of money on something
g) summarise
h) start experiencing difficulties

Hotel Magnifico

Student B

The manager of the Hotel Magnifico received a letter from a customer who wasn't satisfied with her holiday. He replied to the letter. Use these phrasal verbs with *run* to complete the letter.

up • through • over • out of • away • down • into

Hotel Magnifico

Dear Mrs Lott,

Thank you for your letter. It is very rare that we get letters from people who want to run (1) .... our hotel, so we would like to run (2) .... the points you raised one by one.

It is true that a man ran into your husband at the airport, but there is a very simple explanation for this - you'd picked up the wrong suitcase from the carousel. He had your bag and you had his. He was just trying to help you out. So I'm afraid that we will be unable to pay any medical bills that you run (3) ....

You say that some of the buildings near your hotel were run down. You should have read the guidebook. These buildings are, in fact, some of the most famous ancient monuments on the planet. They are 3,500 years old.

You say that several cars were driving on the wrong side of the road. I'd like to point out that we drive on the RIGHT in this country, unlike you in Britain. The reason why you nearly ran (4) .... a pedestrian was that you were driving on the LEFT.

You can run (5) .... problems if you try to make up sentences in a foreign language without knowing any grammar. You looked up some of our words in your pocket dictionary but did you understand exactly what they meant?

You wanted to say, 'I am sick of the food you are serving us' but what you actually said was, 'I have a highly contagious disease picked up from the food you are throwing at me.' So, it's hardly surprising that my staff ran (6) .... Can I suggest you get a better dictionary next time you come to see us?

As for the complimentary salad, we hadn't run (7) .... green salad. It appears you ate the pot pourri.

Yours sincerely

John Rich

Manager - The Hotel Magnifico

Now work in pairs. Match the phrasal verbs and their definitions.

1 run through
2 run over
3 run out of
4 run away
5 run after
6 run up (a bill)
7 run down
8 run into (a problem)

a) chase, follow
b) leave quickly
c) hit someone with a vehicle
d) criticise, allow to deteriorate
e) use something up, have none left
f) spend a lot of money on something
g) summarise
h) start experiencing difficulties

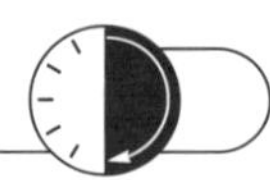

Ask a Silly Question

1. Carina doesn't understand some of the things that her pen-friend, Grimelda, says. Help Carina by matching the idioms with their definitions.

1 sleep like a log
2 smoke like a chimney
3 treat someone like dirt
4 eat like a horse
5 drive like a lunatic
6 get on with someone like a house on fire
7 look like death warmed up
8 spend money like it's going out of fashion

a) very pale / ill
b) madly / wildly
c) really well
d) a lot, continuously
e) freely, without a care
f) soundly / very deeply
g) very badly
h) a lot at one time

2. What advice would you give in these situations?

The Grim Times

1 My best friend smokes like a chimney. How can I get her to give up?

2 My best friend's girlfriend treats him like dirt. It's making him really unhappy.

3 I love shopping, and I'm spending money like it's going out of fashion. How can I stop myself?

4 My father drives like a lunatic. I don't want him to drive me to school anymore. But he insists!

5 I'm really overweight. I eat like a horse – but I can't stop!

6 I sleep like a log and I am frequently late for school.

7 Two of my friends get on like a house on fire. In fact, so much so that I am the one who is left out of everything.

8 I'm worried about my best friend. She says nothing's wrong, but she looks like death warmed up.

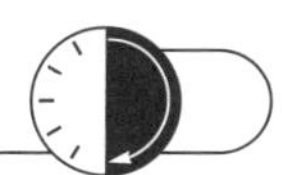

Ask a Silly Question

3. Carina thinks that Grimelda's family is very strange.
Help Grimelda answer Carina's questions by matching the questions to the answers.

1 Why do you have an ashtray on your roof? ☐

2 Why is there a bed in your fireplace? ☐

3 Why is there hay in your dining room? ☐

4 Why do you phone the fire station before your best friend comes round to see you? ☐

5 Why are you afraid of vacuum cleaners? ☐

6 Why is there a psychiatrist in your father's car? ☐

7 Why is there a ghost sitting next to the radiator? ☐

8 Why does your mother keep her cash in the wardrobe? ☐

a) Because she spends money like it's going out of fashion.

b) Because my grandma eats like a horse.

c) Because we get on like a house on fire.

d) Because my father drives like a lunatic.

e) That's my uncle – he looks like death warmed up.

f) Because my granddad smokes like a chimney.

g) Because my sister treats me like dirt.

h) Because my brother sleeps like a log.

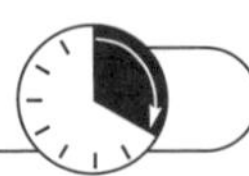

Get Matching

Fill the gaps in section B with the correct prepositions and then match a sentence from A with a sentence from B.

over • round to • at • up • down • away • out of

A

1 I always have a lie-in on Sunday mornings. ☐

2 I hate winter in this part of the world ... the rain, the cold, the snow. ☐

3 Don't be taken in by Maja's little tricks. Look at her now, pretending to be asleep on the sofa. ☐

4 Year in, year out, my brother always buys me the same kind of present for my birthday. ☐

5 I'm really sick of the way my bedroom looks. It's been the same since I was three. ☐

6 Matt has been way from school all week with chicken pox. He's been very ill. ☐

7 Last week Franz got caught shoplifting. He tried to steal a pair of shoes but a couple of security guards stopped him and handed him over to the police. ☐

B

a It's either soap, or shampoo or deodorant. I wonder what he's getting ....?

b He's getting .... it now, though. His spots have gone and he doesn't have to stay in bed.

c She's not really tired. She's just trying to get .... doing the washing up.

d I don't get .... until midday.

e My dad's been promising to redecorate it for ages, but he never gets .... it. I've still got teddy bear wallpaper!

f He just made up some sob story that he was desperately poor. Unbelievably, the police fell for it. I don't know how he gets .... with it!

g The weather here really gets me ....

Ask your partner ...

- What time do you get up at the weekends?
- What gets you down?
- Have you ever told a white lie to get out of doing something you didn't want to do?
- Is there something that you've been meaning to do for a long time but never get round to?
- What things do you sometimes get away with (e.g. not doing your homework)?

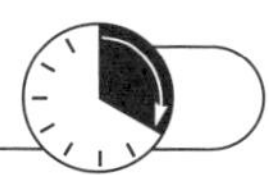

The Health Maze

Go through the maze from the start to the finish by joining up the words or phrases that complete the sentences. If you join them up correctly, you will find the right answer to the question at the end! Take the letters in each square to find the answer. You can go left ←, right → or down ↓ .

1 If you .... with measles your face is covered in red spots.

2 Some people .... in a rash if they eat something they are allergic to.

3 You can sometimes .... to a doctor's surgery for a check-up.

4 If you have a headache, it might help to .... for a while.

5 You .... about an hour after having an operation.

6 A rash may disappear if you .... some cream.

7 If you twist your ankle it can .... quite badly.

8 You get pins and needles if you .... for a long time.

9 An injection can be quite painful at first, but the pain will soon ....

10 If you have toothache, the dentist might have to .... a tooth.

11 If you have a bad fall and can't .... , you might have broken your leg.

START ▼

go down **S**	come out **O**	drop in **R**	look for **A**	call in **R**
come up **O**	call out **L**	lie down **E**	come round **R**	put on **E**
go up **E**	come over **Y**	go out **S**	set on **P**	swell up **D**
fall over **B**	get by **O**	pull out **E**	wear off **Y**	sit down **E**
looked up **R**	emptied out **S**	get up **S**	filled up **T**	topped up **R**

▼ **FINISH**

Question: What complaint can cold teabags cure? .... , ...

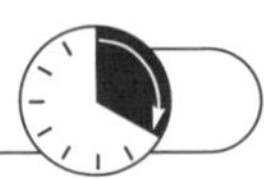

Domino Game with *come*

Instruction for the teacher

Divide the class into small groups. Give each group a shuffled set of dominoes. The students must take turns to arrange the dominoes so that each phrasal verb is next to its definition. They are all correct at present if run on in one continuous line.

The sun comes up every morning.	return
I'm sorry, the library's closed. Can you come back tomorrow?	Where do you come from?
to live in a particular place	I came across these old photographs when I was clearing out a cupboard.
to find by chance	This information is top secret. How did you come by it?
to obtain	Come in!
to enter	She came into a lot of money when her grandfather died.
to inherit	Come off it!
an expression of disbelief	Come on!
an expression of encouragement	The magazine comes out once a month.
to be published	Come round and have a meal with us tomorrow.
to visit someone at their house	The bill came to £100.
to make a total of; add up to	I always come out in a rash when I eat strawberries.
to have an allergic reaction	She came up with a brilliant idea.
to think of	The train came out of the tunnel.
to leave; exit	In the alphabet, B comes after A.
to follow	The old lady came down the stairs very slowly.
to descend	to rise; appear

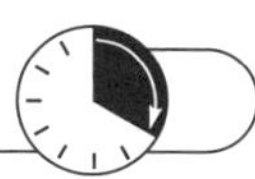

Domino Game with *turn*

Instruction for the teacher

Divide the class into small groups. Give each group a shuffled set of dominoes.
The students must take turns to arrange the dominoes so that each phrasal verb is next to its definition.
They are all correct at present if run on in one continuous line.

The milk's off. I think it's turned into yoghurt!	lower the volume
Could you turn down the radio please?	It's getting late. I think I'll turn in.
to go to bed	They turned down my offer.
to say 'no'; to refuse	Why do you always turn up late?
to arrive	It's too dangerous to keep on swimming. Let's turn back.
to turn around and return to where you came from	I'm bored with this programme. Let's turn over.
to change channels	Can you turn these trousers up for me? They're a bit too long.
to make shorter	He turned out the light and went to sleep.
to switch off	When barbequing meat, turn it over every twenty minutes.
to change the position, so that what was on the bottom is now on top	She turned to me for help.
to ask someone to help you or support you	Everything turned out OK.
to have a result	She turned round when she heard a noise behind her
to move your head to look behind you	I'm going to turn out the bathroom cupboards.
to empty, clean and then tidy	My neighbour's dog suddenly turned on me.
to attack someone without being provoked	She turned the tap on.
to get/make something work	She turned off the motorway at junction 12.
to leave the road	to become; change from one thing to another

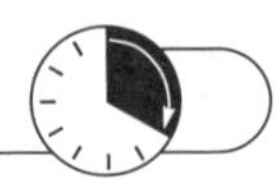

What's the Difference?

Student A

**Find the differences between your picture and your partner's picture.
Fill the gaps in each sentence to find clues.**

1 Elizabeth's really posh; she was born with a silver .... in her mouth.

2 Toby's ever so busy at the moment; he's got a lot on his ....

3 They came to a .... in the road and didn't know which way to go.

4 The news was incredible – you could have knocked me down with a ....

5 Ian is the .... of his mother's eye. She never tells him off for anything.

6 A little .... told me that it's your birthday today. I can't believe you were going to keep it a secret!

7 We don't talk to Emily anymore. She's the black .... of the family.

8 You shouldn't spend a lot of money on things you don't need – money doesn't grow on .... !

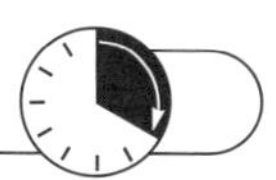

What's the Difference?

Student B

Find the differences between your picture and your partner's picture.
Fill the gaps in each sentence to find clues.

1 He loved skiing from the beginning – he took to it like a .... to water.

2 I've lost my ring. It could be anywhere in the house. It's like looking for a needle in a ....

3 We'll make a lot of money if we sell all the tickets for the school show, but we mustn't count our .... before they're hatched. People might not want to come.

4 Kate has worked all day and gone out every evening this week. She's been burning the .... at both ends.

5 Pete says the rumours aren't true, but I don't believe him. There's no .... without fire.

6 It would be nice to be a teacher instead of a student, but I suppose the .... is always greener on the other side.

7 Emma looks quiet and shy, but you mustn't judge a .... by its cover. She's really outgoing and friendly.

8 I don't know if I'll have enough money for the school trip next year, but I'm not going to worry about it now. I'll cross that .... when I come to it.

What's the Punch-line?

1. Match the phrasal verbs and their definitions.

1 pull over
2 put on (weight)
3 have (someone) in
4 put (someone) up
5 put up with something
6 look into
7 to pick (something) up

a) to get fatter
b) to offer someone a bed
c) to ask someone into your house to do a job
d) to stop your car at the side of the road
e) to learn a skill quickly
f) to suffer something unpleasant
g) to investigate

2. Match the jokes with their punch lines.

1 Two women are standing on a street corner talking when there is a sudden "WHOOSH" sound overhead. They look up and see a phone box flying across the sky. "Wow," says one of the women "Superman's ....

2 Al and Jack are two tramps who sleep rough on the benches in the park. One morning Al comes to Jack and says: "The council are going to paint my bench today. Since I've got the decorators in,

....

3 A woman is driving along the motorway at 200 kilometres per hour. When the police move alongside her car, they notice she is knitting. "Pull over," the police officer says. "No, it's not a pullover" she replies, ...

4 It's the middle of winter, the snow is one metre deep, and Farmer Jones announces that he's going to move his two donkeys into his sitting room. "But what about the smell?" his friend says. "Well," Farmer Jones replies, "The donkeys

....

5 One night a huge hole appears in the Thompsons' front garden. Mrs Thompson goes down to the police station to report it. When she comes home, her husband says "Are the police going to investigate?" "I think so," his wife replies,

....

6 Charlotte gets a detention for talking in class. "Go and collect the litter in the playground," the teacher says. "But I don't know how to collect litter," Charlotte replies, "I've never done it before." "Don't worry," the teacher says,

....

Punch-lines

a) "They say they're going to look into it."
b) "You'll soon pick it up."
c) "I was wondering if you could put me up for the night."
d) ... really put on weight."
e) ... will just have to put up with it."
f) "It's a pair of socks for my nephew."

Body Language

1. Work in pairs. Choose the correct definition for each idiom.

1 to pull someone's leg
a) to play a joke on someone b) to make someone fall over

2 to see eye to eye
a) to be the same height as someone else b) to agree with someone

3 to be up to your eyes in work
a) to find work too difficult b) to have too much work

4 to laugh your head off
a) to laugh a lot b) to be embarrassed

5 to know a place like the back of your hand
a) to be lost b) to know a place very well

6 to have green fingers
a) to be jealous b) to be good at gardening

7 to breathe down someone's neck
a) to give someone a fright b) to watch someone very closely

8 to have cold feet
a) to be anxious about something b) to be confident

2. Now try to find the correct completion for each joke.

1 Why do you walk with a limp?

2 Why didn't the Inuit turn up for his wedding?

3 Why don't you see eye to eye with your brother?

4 Why can't the optician come to our party?

5 Why do you take your gloves off when you get lost?

6 Why do Martians make good gardeners?

7 Why do you wear a scarf in the office?

8 What happens if you tell a joke to a ghost?

A He got cold feet at the last moment and couldn't go through with it.

B Because I know this city like the back of my hand.

C Because she's up to her eyes in work.

D Because they've got green fingers.

E He'll laugh his head off.

F He's 50 centimetres taller than me

G Because the boss is always breathing down my neck.

H Because my sister's always pulling my leg.

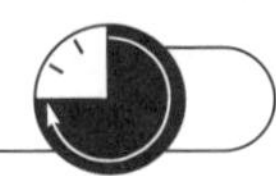

Board Game 2

Instructions for the teacher
Divide the class into groups of four. Each group will need:

- one copy of the board on pages 74 & 75
- one set of idiom cards
- one set of phrasal verb cards
- a die
- a counter for each player

Rules of the game
Player 1 must role the die and move his / her counter the corresponding number of spaces along the board. If the space that they land on has instructions, such as 'Go forward 3' they must do as the instructions say. If they land on a square that says 'phrasal verbs' or 'idioms', another player must pick up a card from the appropriate pile and read out the question on it. If player 1 gives the correct answer, they may role the die again and have another go. If player 1 gives the wrong answer, play passes to the next person. The winner is the first person to get around the board, from beginning to end.

Idioms

"My new computer cost me an arm and a leg." What does it mean?
a) The new computer was expensive.
b) The new computer was cheap.
c) The new computer was stolen.

Answer: The new computer was expensive

If everything runs like clockwork, what happens?
a) Everything happens on time.
b) Everything happens late.
c) Everything happens exactly as planned.

Answer: Everything happens exactly as planned

"This restaurant is really going to the dogs." What's happening to the restaurant?
a) It's getting worse.
b) It's getting better.
c) It allows pets.

Answer: It's getting worse

"He's a vegetarian. So, I really put my foot in it when I offered him a ham sandwich." What did I do?
a) I trod on the sandwich.
b) I made a mistake.
c) I apologised.

Answer: I make a mistake

"I couldn't keep a straight face when his wig fell off." What happened?
a) I couldn't help laughing.
b) I couldn't help crying.
c) I couldn't help him put his wig back on.

Answer: I couldn't help laughing

"That job is right up your street." What does it mean?
a) The job is near where you live.
b) It's a job you do outside.
c) It's the perfect job for you.

Answer: It's the perfect job for you

"He got out of bed the wrong side this morning." What does it mean?
a) He's in a bad mood.
b) He's got his jumper on inside out.
c) He's tired.

Answer: He's in a bad mood

"She's got her head in the clouds." What's she like?
a) She's very tall.
b) She's very ambitious.
c) She's always day-dreaming.

Answer: She's always day-dreaming

"He's down in the dumps at the moment." What does it mean?
a) He's in the basement.
b) He's throwing out the rubbish.
c) He's depressed.

Answer: He's depressed

"I feel better now that I've got that off my chest." What did I do?
a) I asked for forgiveness.
b) I said what was on my mind.
c) I kept a secret.

Answer: I said what was on my mind

She's rolling in money. What does it mean?
a) She's rich.
b) She's poor.
c) She's dreaming of being rich.

Answer: She's rich

"There's no love lost between them" What does it mean?
a) They love each other.
b) They hate each other.
c) They are both in love with the same person.

Answer: They hate each other

It's raining cats and dogs. What's the weather like?
a) It's raining heavily.
b) It's raining lightly.
c) It's hardly raining at all.

Answer: It's raining heavily

He buys me flowers once in a blue moon. How often does he buy me flowers?
a) He often buys me flowers.
b) He rarely buys me flowers.
c) He buys me flowers on my birthday.

Answer: He rarely buys me flowers

He's a big cheese. What's he like?
a) He's smelly.
b) He's very important.
c) He loves cheese.

Answer: He's very important

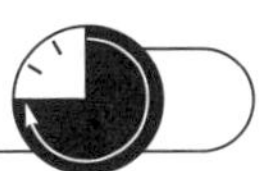

Board Game 2

Phrasal Verbs

What might you give up when you go on a diet?
a) exercise
b) fruit
c) cake

Answer: cake

If you arrange to go out with someone and they stand you up, what do they do?
a) They arrive too early.
b) They arrive too late.
c) They don't arrive at all.

Answer: They don't arrive at all

"I bought the ticket from a ticket tout. He really ripped me off." What happened?
a) I paid too much for the ticket.
b) The ticket was cheap.
c) The ticket wasn't genuine.

Answer: I paid too much for the ticket

"He really looks up to his brother." What does it mean?
a) He is shorter than his brother.
b) He respects his brother.
c) He is scared of his brother.

Answer: He respects his brother

"They let her off paying the fine." What happened?
a) She had to pay the fine.
b) She didn't have to pay the fine.
c) She was in trouble for not paying the fine.

Answer: She didn't have to pay the fine

"He looks down on poor people." What does he think of poor people?
a) He feels sorry for poor people.
b) He thinks we should help poor people.
c) He doesn't respect poor people.

Answer: He doesn't respect poor people

"My computer was playing up all day yesterday." What does it mean?
a) My computer worked perfectly all day.
b) My computer kept going wrong.
c) I was playing computer games all day.

Answer: My computer kept going wrong

She's winding you up. What's she doing?
a) She's trying to make you angry.
b) She's trying to make you smile.
c) She's trying to make you feel calmer.

Answer: She's trying to make you angry

"They've fallen out over money." What have they done?
a) They've had an argument.
b) They've hurt themselves.
c) They've spent too much money.

Answer: They've had an argument

"I give in." What does it mean?
a) I'm giving you a present.
b) I'm inviting you to my house.
c) I'm going to stop trying.

Answer: I'm going to stop trying

What can you take up if you want to get fit?
a) acting
b) a musical instrument
c) a sport, like tennis or football

Answer: a sport, like tennis or football

If you put by money, what do you do with it?
a) You spend it.
b) You save it.
c) You hide it.

Answer: You save it

If you pop in to see someone, what do you do?
a) You pay someone a quick visit.
b) You climb into someone's house through a window.
c) You drive by someone's house, but you don't stop.

Answer: You pay someone a quick visit

"I messed up my exam." What happened?
a) I didn't go to my exam.
b) I did badly in my exam.
c) I did well in my exam.

Answer: I did badly in my exam

"I take after my dad." What does it mean?
a) I go everywhere with my dad.
b) I make jokes about my dad.
c) I'm similar to my dad in some way.

Answer: I'm similar to my dad in some way

Animal Behaviour

**Fill the gaps in the sentences with the correct animals.
The pictures will help you.**

1 My brother's like a .... in a china shop. He's really clumsy.

2 Without my glasses, I can't see anything. I'm as blind as a ....

3 My sister and I fight like .... and ....

4 Don't trust Monique. Nothing she says is true. She's a real .... in the grass.

5 My sister's really grumpy, especially first thing in the morning. She's like a .... with a sore head when she gets up.

6 Marie cried when she broke up with her boyfriend, but she wasn't really upset – they were .... tears.

7 Jean Luc loves food, but he eats like a ....

8 We got stuck in an awful traffic jam yesterday. The car hardly moved at all for an hour. We were travelling at a ....'s pace.

9 My brother and I baked a cake for my mum's birthday. I did all the .... work. He only put the candles on the cake.

10 If you keep making a fuss about little things, no one will take you seriously when something goes wrong. You know what happened to the boy who cried ....

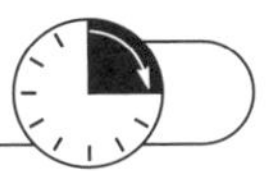

Dinner Time

Look at the food and drink in the picture and use ten of the items to complete the sentences below. One item in the picture is not used in the sentences. Which one?

1 Riding a bike is easy. It's a piece of ....

2 I've never really taken to opera. It's just a lot of odd people wandering around shouting at each other. It's not my cup of ....

3 My uncle's a couch .... and he's always glued to the TV.

4 André suffers from terrible road rage. If another driver cuts him up or pulls out in front of him, he just goes ....

5 Michel looks as if .... wouldn't melt in his mouth, but don't be taken in by him. I wouldn't trust him an inch. He's a wolf in sheep's clothing.

6 Ana was standing in a queue at the bank when two robbers burst in and held up the staff. Some of the customers started screaming but Ana was as cool as a .... She took out her mobile phone and called the police.

7 Elena thinks her new WAP phone is the best thing since sliced ....

8 I turned up at a party last night wearing jeans and a t-shirt. Everyone else was dressed formally. I felt like a .... out of water.

9 Pierre works on the checkout at her local supermarket. They pay him ....

10 What does Sabine mean, she didn't want to win the art competition?! She spent ages doing her project! I think it's just sour .... on her part. She's jealous, because someone else won instead of her.

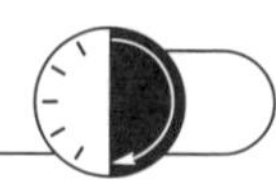

Fact or Fiction?

Decide whether the following sentences are true or false. Write the letter next to your answer in the boxes below. If your answers are right, you will find the name of a SNAKE, a FRUIT and a COUNTRY.

		True	False
1	A sheep dog chases after sheep	A	P
2	A sausage dog looks after sausages	S	N
3	A nervous cow is called a milkshake	F	A
4	A windpipe is part of your body	C	G
5	A gas pipe is part of your body	Z	O
6	You can eat traffic jam	U	N
7	A king that likes to go fishing is called a kingfisher	W	D
8	An aeroplane lands on a runway	A	B
9	A clock has hands	B	S
10	A table has legs	A	L
11	You can catch a train at a power station	O	N
12	You can milk a cow	A	U
13	You can write a letter with a penknife	X	N
14	A penny has two sides: "heads" and "feet"	T	A
15	A river has a mouth	C	G
16	A tea bag is full of tea leaves	A	R
17	A tea cake is full of tea leaves	Y	N
18	You serve food on a number plate	P	A
19	Day breaks	D	I
20	Night falls	A	V

(answers 1 to 8) The snake is an ☐☐☐☐☐☐☐☐

(answers 9 to 14) The fruit is a ☐☐☐☐☐☐

(answers 15 to 20) The country is ☐☐☐☐☐☐

Criminal Quiz

See if you can answer the questions in this quiz about people and their relationships. You will find clues by matching one picture to each question.

1 Who does a bully pick on? Someone weaker or stronger than themselves? ....

2 The jewel thief got away with the crime. Was the jewel thief punished or not? ....

3 The police are cracking down on joyriders. Does this mean the police are now making more effort or less effort to stamp out joyriding? ....

4 My cousin was beaten up by a couple of thugs yesterday. Who was injured, my cousin or the thugs? ....

5 The policewoman let me off with a warning. Did I have to go to court or not? ....

6 Someone broke into the factory last night. Did the thief use a key to get in? ....

7 The mugger ran off with my wallet. Does a mugger steal things secretively? ....

8 The tout wanted £100 for the concert ticket. I told him he was ripping me off. Did I think it was a fair price? ....

9 "Do you want to buy a video recorder, brand new, for £20? I've got ten of them for sale; they all fell off the back of a lorry!" Were the videos stolen? ....

10 They've done away with speed limits on German motorways. Does this mean you can drive as fast as you want now? ....

11 Someone tipped the police off that the robbers were going to hold up the security van. Were the police at the scene of the crime by chance? ....

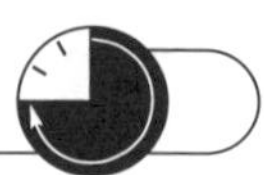

True Stories?

a) **Look at the stories and facts below. For each of the numbers 1 to 13 you have to decide if the information is true or false. Choosing the correct definition for the phrasal verb in the box will help you do this!**

b) **All of the stories contain more phrasal verbs. How many phrasal verbs can you find?**

c) **How many of the phrasal verbs can you replace with other verbs? For example in number 2, *If you are having problems* <u>*picking up*</u> *English* changes to *If you are having problems* <u>*learning*</u> *English.***

1 Two groups of scientists working for the *Du Pont Chemical Company* claimed that they had come up with the idea for a new material first. There was an argument about who should be credited with the discovery and neither the scientists in New York nor the scientists in London would [back down.] To make sure that the two groups didn't fall out, the *Du Pont Company* reached a compromise and called the new material NY (for New York) + LON (for London), or NYLON.

True **(no longer keep to your position in an argument)**
False **(do as promised)**

2 If you feel that you're having problems picking up English, then don't despair! Although English has more words in it than any other language (it is made up of approximately a million different words) most English people [get by] using only 1 per cent of the words available.

True **(just manage)**
False **(struggle)**

3 When Adelaide Simpson moved into the White House in 1871 (he was the first President to live there) he wanted the house painted in the three colours of the American flag, (red, white and blue). However, when the builders turned up they told the President that the local shops in Washington had [run out of] red and blue paint and they only had white paint left in stock. So the President reluctantly gave in and had the whole building painted white, and within a few days the President's official residence became known as the "White House".

True **(just bought)**
False **(not have any left)**

4 A farmer decided to sell his horse. The new owner, a businessman, wanted to give the horse a different name and he asked the farmer if he could [come up with] any ideas. "Well, I gave up trying to train this horse a long time ago," the farmer said, "This is a horse that makes you so angry that some days you feel like you want to murder it, so why don't you call the horse 'murder', that would be just right." The businessman decided that "murder" was not a very suitable name for a horse, so he turned the word around and called the horse "Red Rum" which is "muR-deR" spelt backwards. In the 1980s, Red Rum became the only horse to win Britain's most important race, the Grand National, three times.

True **(think of)**
False **(leave)**

5 When the Michigan Toy Company brought out their first toy bears in 1906, they named them after the American President Theodore (or Teddy for short) Roosevelt. The President had famously [turned down] an invitation to go bear-hunting because he thought it was a cruel sport. "I'm a friend of all the bears in all the woods of America," he said. And that's why toy bears are known as "teddy bears" or "teddies".

True **(refuse, reject)**
False **(accept)**

6 People in Europe and the USA now [polish off] about 20 times as much sugar and at least 5 times as much fat as they did in 1800. This may be why the number of people with heart disease has gone up so dramatically in western countries.

True **(consume)**
False **(buy)**

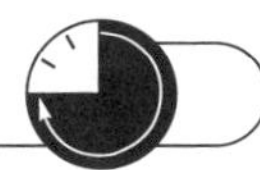

True Stories?

7 In 1876 a group of boys were playing football at a school called Rugby in central England. One of the boys, 16-year-old William Webb Ellis, picked the ball up and ran with it across the pitch. Over the next few weeks this new tactic caught on among the boys and that's how rugby was born.

True **(become popular)**
False **(discover)**

8 Policewoman Jenny Paterson got a message on her police radio and spent the afternoon of 7th March 2001 looking into the theft of a saxophone from a school. Although it wasn't a serious crime, she didn't want the thieves to get away with it. When she got back to the police station she had to put up with a lot of teasing from her colleagues. The thief had actually stolen a fax and phone from the school. "There was a lot of noise in the street when I took the message," Officer Paterson said "and I couldn't make out what the station were saying to me. It was an easy mistake to make."

True **(see or hear clearly)**
False **(pretend)**

9 The inventor Alexander Graham Bell made the first telephone call in 1832 when he connected a phone in his office to a second phone in his kitchen. When he finally got through to his wife in the kitchen he told her, "I'm fed up with salads and I'm not going to eat them any more. If I eat one more piece of lettuce I'll turn into a rabbit." Unsurprisingly, his wife hung up on him and they split up a few months later.

True **(have an argument)**
False **(end a phone conversation)**

10 The Beatles, the world's most successful pop group, were turned down by the first four record companies they approached. The record companies said that guitar music wouldn't take off with young people.

True **(become popular)**
False **(lose popularity)**

11 In 1782, the King of England (George III) found out that every morning, the Queen slipped out of the back door of Buckingham Palace and met her lover in Green Park, just 100 metres away. On her walk through the park the Queen would stop and pick flowers for her lover. The King couldn't get over it and he was mad with jealousy. The King ordered that all the flowers in Green Park should be pulled up and thrown away and he told his gardeners never to plant any more flowers in Green Park from that moment on. Two hundred years later, the tradition still lives on and Green Park is the only major park in London without any flowers.

True **(accept)**
False **(believe)**

12 The steel used to build the first railway system in Russia was made in an area of south London called Vauxhall. The steel was transported from London to Moscow in large crates with the word "Vauxhall" on the side and the word was soon picked up by the Russian workmen who were putting down the track. In time, "Vauxhall" caught on as part of the general language and that's why "vokzál" is the Russian word for "railway".

True **(learn without much effort)**
False **(despise)**

13 The modern name for the highest mountain in the world, Mount Everest, comes from a joke made by a Canadian explorer called Francis Guillardot who made one of the first attempts to climb Everest in 1911. Previously, the mountain was known as K-21. A few hours before Guillardot set off on his 8,836-metre climb, a young newspaper journalist asked him: "What will be the first thing you do, Sir, when you get to the top of this great mountain?" Guillardot smiled and said: "Have a rest." K-21 became known as the "Have a rest" mountain and, over time, "Have a rest" turned into "Everest", the name we use today.

True **(prepare for)**
False **(leave on a journey)**

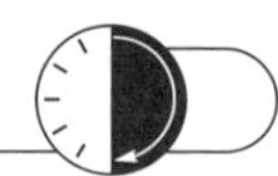

The Perfect Job

**Are you a goalkeeper, a book-keeper or a beekeeper?
What sort of job would suit you? Would road sweeping be right up your street?
Would waitressing be your cup of tea? Would you be on cloud nine working as a pilot?
Find out by answering the job quiz below!**

Answer the questions below choosing a, b or c. Tick the picture next to your answer. Then see the box below to discover what sort of job would really suit you.

1 You have to make a speech in front of a large group of people. What do you do?

a) stay as cool as a cucumber and just get on with it  ☐

b) get butterflies in your stomach but still go through with it  ☐

c) go as red as a beetroot and run away  ☐

2 You are offered a great job in another country. But if you take up the job you'll need to learn a new language from scratch. What do you do?

a) jump at the chance and start preparing   ☐

b) ask if you can put off a decision for a year or two while you weigh up the pros and cons  ☐

c) turn down the job because it would be too much hassle   ☐

3 What are you like with money?

a) You think that money grows on trees  ☐

b) You like to put by money every month, saving for a rainy day  ☐

c) You're tight-fisted. Getting money out of you is like getting blood out of a stone ☐

4 You win a prize in a competition: you get a free bungee jump from a platform 100 metres off the ground, without a safety net. What do you do?

a) jump for joy and go for it ☐

b) come up with a compromise, how about 50 metres with a safety net? 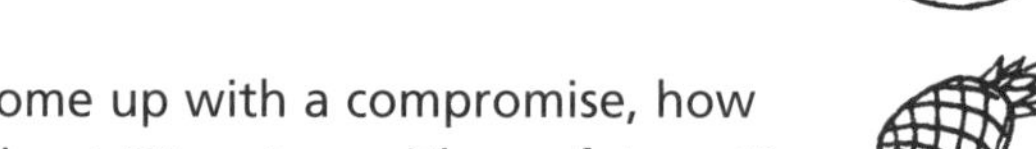 ☐

c) turn down the offer saying 'Anyone who bungee jumps is one sandwich short of a picnic!' 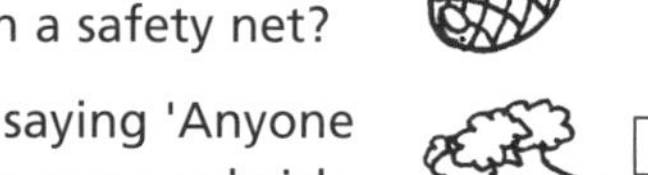 ☐

5 What sort of holiday would you prefer?

a) mountain climbing, white-water rafting, camping off the beaten track  ☐

b) a long lie-in followed by gentle hill walking and boat trips around the bay  ☐

c) two weeks at home, and a chance to put your feet up. You'd catch up on all those TV programmes you videoed but never got round to watching  ☐

What your answers mean:

Mainly sweet things
You're generous and sociable, the life and soul of the party. You get on well with people from all walks of life and a job that involves contact with people would be right up your street. You want to change the world and be the centre of attention. Think of a career as: an actor, a tour guide, a television presenter, a flight attendant, a politician, a goalkeeper.

Mainly fruit
You want a job with loads of responsibility. You're cautious and sensible and don't like taking risks. You look before you leap and never put all your eggs in one basket. Careful planning will help you weather a storm. You don't like to rock the boat, you want to know where you stand. These jobs would suit you perfectly: a doctor, a judge, a traffic warden, a bank manager, a book-keeper.

Mainly vegetables
You like the simple life, nothing too strenuous. A regular 9-5 job would suit you down to the ground. You don't really like planning ahead, you play it by ear and go with the flow. You take things one day at a time, and although you get on well with people you keep yourself to yourself and don't mind working alone. So, think about a job as: an athlete, a painter, a lighthouse keeper, a zookeeper, a beekeeper.

The Perfect Job

Go through the maze from the start to the finish by joining up the words or phrases that complete these sentences. If you join them up correctly, you will find the right answer to the question at the end. Take the letters in each square to find the answer. You can go left ←, right → or down ↓.

1 as cool as a cucumber = ...
2 If you're nervous, you have .... in your stomach
3 If you go as red as a beetroot, you ....
4 From .... means 'from the very beginning'.
5 If you delay things, you .... them ....
6 advantages and disadvantages = ...
7 to save regularly = ...
8 to be mean with money = ...
9 to turn down (an offer) = ...
10 off the beaten track = ...
11 to put your feet up = ...
12 Don't put all your .... in one basket.
13 To get through difficult times is to weather the ....
14 To make trouble is to rock the ....
15 to improvise = play it by ....

START ↓ (above "calm")

calm F	ants R	put O	call off N	say yes U	deserted E	read N
butterflies L	blush I	scratch G	put on P	left handed L	reply O	uninhabited L
cry A	itch F	put off H	pros and cons T	put by A	tight-fisted T	accept J
tear T	eye S	ups and downs S	put up E	half hearted B	say no T	populated M
head E	boat N	storm A	eggs D	relax N	isolated E	exercise G
arm O	ear T	ship R	rain O	pies U	die N	cakes T

FINISH ↓ (below "ear")

What is Irma's job?

She's a _ _ _ _ _ _ _ _ _ _ _ _ _ _ _ _ _

Super Grid: UP

Use the words below to complete the Super Grid for phrasal verbs with the particle UP.

break
build
cheer
clear
do
eat
give
grow
look
put
save
speak
stay
tidy
use
wash

1	c	l	e	a	r	u	p
2						u	p
3						u	p
4						u	p
5						u	p
6						u	p
7						u	p
8						u	p
9						u	p
10						u	p
11						u	p
12						u	p
13						u	p
14						u	p
15						u	p
16						u	p

Super Grid: UP

1 Put some cream on the rash. It'll soon .... up.

2 I put by a little money every week. I'm trying to .... up for a new bike.

3 The weightlifter does special exercises to .... up his muscles.

4 You're bedroom's a mess. You'd better .... it up, NOW!

5 Shall we .... up and watch the late film?

6 Soon after I was born, my family went to live in a small fishing village in the south of Portugal. It was a beautiful place to .... up.

7 .... up! I can't hear what you're saying.

8 I think we'd better .... up. We're the only people left in the restaurant and the staff look as if they want to go home.

9 My brother's really fed up at the moment. He failed his driving test and he's really down in the dumps. I wonder what I can do to .... him up?

10 My sister's so selfish. She spends hours in the bathroom. How can someone .... up all the hot water like that and not care about anyone else?

11 I've bought a new dishwasher. It's great. I don't have to .... up any more.

12 If you know the answer to the question, ... up your hand.

13 If you don't know the meaning of a word, ... it up.

14 When the bus is full, please .... up your seat if an elderly person gets on.

15 .... up your coat. It's getting chilly.

16 Why does my mobile phone always .... up when we drive through a tunnel?

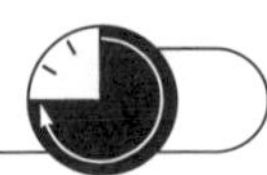

Super Grid: DOWN

Use the words below to complete the Super Grid for phrasal verbs with the particle DOWN. (If you need help, you'll find the letters of the verbs in the underlined words in the sentences.)

- slow
- go
- lie
- get
- calm
- bring
- live
- wind
- let
- run
- turn
- put
- live
- hang
- knock

1		s	l	o	w	d	o	w	n
2						d	o	w	n
3						d	o	w	n
4						d	o	w	n
5						d	o	w	n
6						d	o	w	n
7						d	o	w	n
8						d	o	w	n
9						d	o	w	n
10						d	o	w	n
11						d	o	w	n
12						d	o	w	n
13						d	o	w	n
14						d	o	w	n

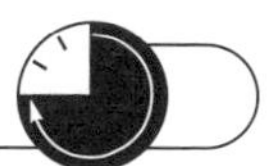

Super Grid: DOWN

1 Mr Wolsley, my next door neighbour, drives much too fast. If he doesn't ...*slow*... down he's going to have an accident.

2 Our cat, Mister Purrfect, got very sick this summer, so we had to have him .... down.

3 Bridget took up golf last week but it's not as easy as it looks. She can't hit the ball. She was a bit disappointed. "Be patient," I said. "Don't let it .... you down."

4 Malcolm gets very anxious when he has to do an exam. He needs to relax more, take it easy, just .... down.

5 Why don't you come and stay with us at our holiday house in Brighton? There's lots of room, so you can .... some of your friends down if you like.

6 Melanie was feeling a bit dizzy just now, so she's gone to .... down.

7 "You'll have a bump on your head," Dr Gopil said. "But don't worry, it'll soon .... down."

8 How can you .... down Australia? It's a fantastic county and Melbourne is a wonderful city.

9 Colonel James is a guard at Windsor Castle. When he gets home after work, he likes to run a bath, add some bubble bath, take the phone off the hook, get in the water, stretch out and close his eyes. "It's the best way to .... down after a hard day's work," he says.

10 They're going to .... down the old fire station in Kilmarnock and put up a multi-storey car park.

11 I wanted to sign up for an advanced Italian language course at Turin University but when I told them that I only know three words in Italian (*pizza*, *spaghetti* and *ravioli*) they decided to .... me down.

12 When Oliver appeared on a TV quiz programme last week, the first question they asked him was, "And what's your name, contestant number three?" Oliver's mind went a complete blank. "I don't know," he said, "I can't remember!" Later, he said, "I'll never .... this down."

13 Colette is the most reliable person I know. She always keeps her word and she'll never .... you down.

14 A few kilometres outside Shanghai there are some ancient caves. Over thousands of years, water has seeped down from the ground above and now there are enormous stalactites, 50 metres long, that .... down from the walls of the caves.

Super Grid

Now use this blank grid to make your own Super Grid.

1 Choose a preposition to enter into each square of the grid, e.g. *into, out, in, on, away.* **Do not write any verbs in your grid**.

2 Write as many sentences as you can in **'My Sentences'** with verbs which combine with the preposition you have chosen. Instead of writing the verbs, leave them out.

3 Your teacher will make copies of your grid to give to other pairs or groups.

4 When you have completed the grid your teacher gives you, hand it back to the student who wrote it, for checking.

	Verb	Preposition
1		
2		
3		
4		
5		
6		
7		
8		
9		
10		
11		
12		
13		
14		

My Sentences

1 ....

2 ....

3 ....

4 ....

5 ....

6 ....

7 ....

8 ....

9 ....

10 ....

11 ....

12 ....

13 ....

14 ....

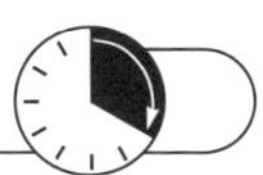

Idiom Crossword

Complete the crossword with the missing words from the idioms. Each word is connected with geography or the weather.

Clues across

1 It's mum's 40th birthday next week. She says she's over the ...., but 40 isn't that old.

4 We did a geography exam today. The first question was, 'How many people live in Birmingham?' How could I know something like that? I haven't a clue – I haven't the .... idea!

7 I've got so much homework to do for next week – I'm completely ....ed under.

10 Monika is doing really badly at school, but she won't admit there's a problem. She's burying her head in the ....

11 Eva's really dreading the test on Friday, but she's good at maths and it isn't a real exam. She's making a .... out of a molehill.

Clues down

2 Karolina is very outgoing. She isn't afraid to go up to people and talk about herself. She certainly breaks the .... at parties.

3 Erika won a skiing holiday in a competition. She was over the ....

5 The new shopping centre in town is amazing. You can buy anything there. It's got everything under the ....

6 I twisted my ankle yesterday and I'm going to be laid up in bed for a couple of days. My ankle is really sore, but at least I get out of going to school for a while. Every .... has a silver lining.

7 Stop making such a big fuss about your argument with Klaus. It's not very important. It's just a .... in a teacup.

8 Steffi has got a part-time job and she puts by £5 a week. She's saving it for a .... day.

9 My new bike is fantastic – it's really fast. It goes like the ....!

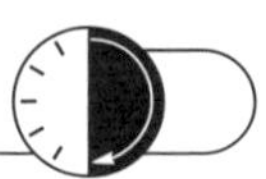

Clowns International

1. Match the phrasal verbs to their definitions

1	go on	**A**	to establish an organisation
2	carry out	**B**	to prepare to do something
3	crop up	**C**	to register
4	find out	**D**	to happen
5	give up	**E**	to get information
6	hit upon (a solution)	**F**	to appear, often suddenly and unexpectedly
7	put on (a show)	**G**	to do something as arranged or promised
8	put on (make-up)	**H**	to sacrifice something
9	set out	**I**	to perform
10	set up	**K**	to have a new idea
11	sign up	**L**	to apply cosmetics

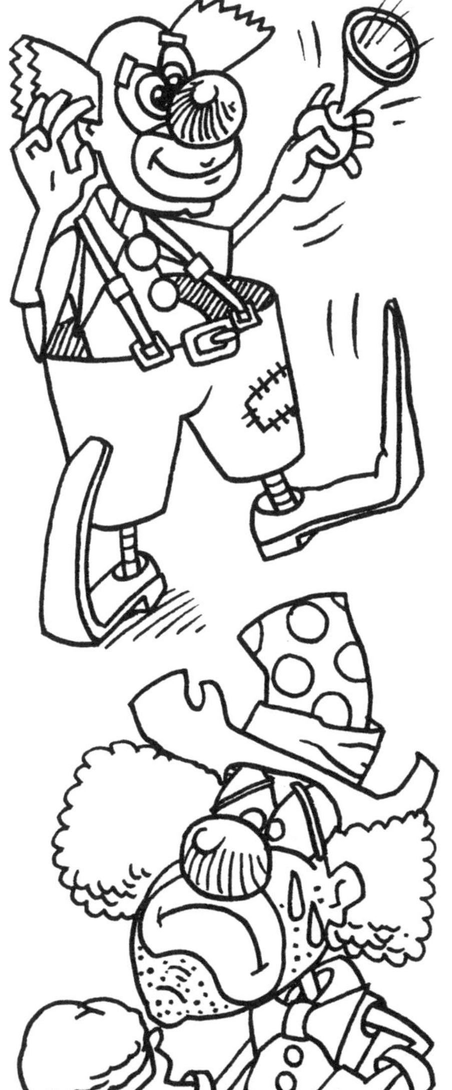

2. Use the phrasal verbs to complete the text. You will have to use the present continuous form in some places.

CLOWNS INTERNATIONAL

Have you ever noticed how every clown looks different, with his or her own unique look and costume? Well, there's a reason for this. Welcome to the world of Clowns International.

In 1947, a man called Stan Bult 1 .... an organisation called 'The International Circus Clowns Club', later known as "Clowns International".

"What we 2 .... to do in those early days," Burt said, "was to bring the world community of clowns together in some way, so that performers from different countries could share experiences with each other, swap stories and keep up to date with what was 3 .... in the clown world.

But we soon discovered that when clowns got together to talk about their profession there was one problem that kept on 4 ...., and that was how angry performers got when other clowns copied their 'slap' and 'motley' (the clown words for 'make-up' and 'costume').

"It's a complete rip-off," one clown said "Every time I come up with a new design for my 'motley' or a different way of 5 .... my 'slap', someone steals the idea from right under my nose and does exactly the same thing as me."

But how could a clown copyright his or her look? How could you stop two clowns looking the same?

Clowns International

After weeks of discussion, Bult 6 .... a simple solution. He decided to start a Slap and Motley Register, and he asked members of the clown club to 7........................ .... Once registered, a clown's look was unique and couldn't be copied by anyone else.

Once a clown has chosen their individual slap and motley, the look is registered and painted on an eggshell at the headquarters of Clowns International in East London.

So that's why, since the 1950s, no two have been the same.

To find out more, log on to their website at www.clowns-international.co.uk where you can see pictures of the eggshell faces, and 8 .... more about the ways in which many clowns 9 .... their free time to help others by 10 .... charity work, such as visiting sick children in hospitals or 11 .... shows at youth clubs and old people's homes.

Role play

Student A

You want to set up an organisation or business. You want to convince your bank manager, **Student B**, that you've hit upon a great idea so that he / she will lend you some money. But the bank manager isn't going to be easy to persuade. What are you going to do to make sure this business is a success? The phrasal verbs below will help you.

take off
set up
set out
build up
sell out
branch out

Student B

You are a bank manager. **Student A** wants you to lend him / her some money to set up an organisation or business. You feel very doubtful that it will take off. You've seen lots of ideas like this fall through in the past. Try to dissuade him / her from setting up the organisation. The phrasal verbs below will help you.

think over
fall through
cut back
lay off
take over
go under
dry up

Pocahontas

Complete the text with the phrasal verbs below.
There are questions in the text for you to discuss as a class.

set off (to begin a journey)
set off (to trigger a reaction)
set up (to organise)
set upon (to attack)
set in (to begin)
set about (to start a task)
set out (to have the intention of doing something)

break out
try on
give in
make of
put out

burn down
pick up
cut (someone) off
come across
name after

The story of Pocahontas and the English

400 years ago, hundreds of British people boarded ships in the western English ports of Plymouth and Bristol and 1 .... off on a 5000 km journey across the Atlantic Ocean to start a new life on the east coast of America, the area we now call Virginia.

The people who took this journey had different reasons for leaving Britain. Some were fleeing from religious persecution, some were evangelists hoping to convert the Native Americans to Christianity, others had heard of the extraordinary natural resources of the New World (gold, silver, sugar, jewels) and were hoping to make their fortune.

Question: In an age before newspapers, television, photographs and the Internet, what do you think people imagined the New World of the Americas would be like? Remember at this time many people thought that the world was flat and that if you travelled too far you would fall off the edge.

When the first settlers arrived from England, they decided to build a small town near the Atlantic coast, which they would call Jamestown, 2 .... after the new English King, James 1st.

The building of Jamestown began just hours after the first colonists arrived. There was no time to lose because the early settlers had travelled in the autumn and they knew that when winter 3 .... in they would effectively be cut off from the outside world.

The settlers started by clearing the land and constructing rough wooden shacks, but there was a huge setback just days after the work began when some of these buildings 4 .... down. The settlers refused to 5 .... in and as soon as the fire was 6 .... out they 7 .... about building the shacks again.

To get wood and other resources for their houses, the settlers moved onto the lands that Native American tribes lived on, and it wasn't long before there were violent clashes between the two groups.

"We didn't 8 .... out to fight the Indians," one settler wrote, "it just happened that way. And now, the fighting feeds upon itself. We attack them, they 9 .... upon us, and this 10 .... off a chain reaction of more fighting and more anger. It's just a vicious circle."

Question: How do you think the Native Americans felt when they saw the newcomers beginning to build Jamestown on the land they lived on?

It was near Jamestown, in 1607, that Pocahontas, the 12-year-old daughter of the leader of the Algonquin tribes of Indians, first came across the settlers from Europe.

Despite the fighting, she decided to go into Jamestown and bring the colonists food. The settlers were so taken

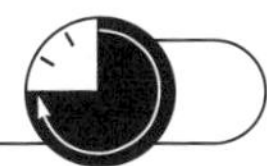

Pocahontas

by this gesture, that they welcomed her into their houses. "It was wonderful," Pocahontas said, "to see so many new things. They let me 11 .... on their clothes and I managed to 12 .... up a few words of their strange language called English."

Soon after Pocahontas had made her first contact with the settlers, the Algonquians captured a colonist called John Smith. While they were deciding whether he should be killed, Pocahontas stood in front of Smith and put her head on his shoulder. She was saying that the Indians should spare his life, even though he was their enemy. Touched by her actions, they agreed to set him free, and Pocahontas now decided she should act as a kind of bridge between the two communities, even though it would put her in real danger.

Questions: What kind of arguments do you imagine Pocahontas used to try and bring the two communities together? What do you think she said to her father, Chief Powhatan? What do you think she said to the settlers?

In 1608, there was more fighting, and the colonists held several Native Americans prisoner in Jamestown. When Pocahontas heard about this, she 13 .... up a meeting between her father and the settlers and encouraged the two sides to make peace. After hours of discussion the prisoners were set free.

But the peace didn't last long and a year later, in 1609, a full-scale war 14 .... out. The war would last for five years. There was nothing Pocahontas could do and she lost contact with many of her settler friends. And then, in 1613, things went from bad to worse.

Pocahontas was kidnapped by the colonists. Chief Powhatan was told that the only way he could get his daughter back was to end the war but he refused to give in to this blackmail and the fighting continued.

Question: Was Chief Powhatan right to keep on fighting? Should he have made peace in order to get his daughter back?

The colonists 15 .... Pocahontas off from her family and held her prisoner. In 1614, when she was 19, she converted to Christianity and married one of the settlers, a man called John Rolfe.

She took a new name, Rebecca, and because of her marriage, she was now free to see her father and family again. Somehow, finally, she managed to get the two sides to stop fighting.

Soon after, Pocahontas gave birth to a son, Thomas. In 1616, her husband decided to return to England and he persuaded her to go with him.

Her visit to England caused a sensation. None of the English people she met had ever 16 .... across a Native American before and they were fascinated by her. When she met King James, for example, he called her a "woman of wondrous beauty".

Questions: How do you think the marriage between the daughter of Chief Powhatan and one of the settlers changed the relationship between the Indians and the colonists? What do you think Pocahontas 17 .... of England?

In March 1617, a few months after she arrived in England, Pocahontas fell ill. She decided to go back to America and boarded a ship bound for Virginia but before the boat had reached the open sea, a doctor told her she was too sick to travel. She got off the boat and died a few days later, in a village 30 kilometres from London. She was just 22.

Question: What can we learn from the life of Pocahontas?

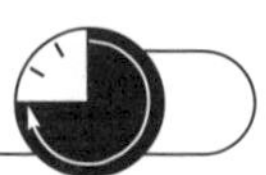

Pocahontas

Put the pictures below into the right order, adding a preposition to complete the phrasal verb.

a) When Pocahontas was kidnapped, her father was told to stop the war if he wanted to see his daughter again. But he refused to give .... to blackmail.

b) In 1609, war broke .... between the colonists and the Algonquians.

c) Pocahontas's captors cut her .... from her family.

d) Some of the houses the settlers built burned ....

e) In 1608, Pocahontas set .... a meeting between her father and the settlers.

f) When Pocahontas visited Jamestown, she enjoyed trying .... the strange clothes of the settlers.

g) Four centuries ago, hundreds of British people set .... for the New World.

h) Pocahontas first came .... the settlers in 1607.

i) The town that the settlers built was named .... King James.

Colour Codes

Find your way through the maze by finding the missing words. Move one square at a time. You can move left ←, right →, or down ↓.

START ▼

blue	red	blue	orange	yellow	pink
blue	brown	grey	white	green	red
red	pink	brown	orange	yellow	blue
orange	green	silver	red	blue	black
red	white	grey	white	brown	yellow
orange	pink	mauve	red	blue	red

▼ FINISH (below pink)

1 My best friend swears she's related to the Queen. She thinks she's got .... blood.

2 He's so shy. When a girl spoke to him on the bus yesterday he went as .... as a beetroot.

3 You can shout at him until you're .... in the face but you'll never get him to tidy up his room.

4 Is it right to eat meat? I don't know. It isn't a black and white issue. There are lots of .... areas.

5 Why didn't she come out with us yesterday? She said she was going to stay home and have an early night but I don't believe her. I think she was telling us a .... lie.

6 He's got a fantastic new DVD player. I'm .... with envy.

7 The test was really difficult. I think that there were a few trick questions. Some of them definitely looked like .... herrings.

8 I really wasn't expecting your letter. It came out of the ....

9 We don't talk to my cousin any more. She's the .... sheep of the family.

10 I hardly ever see Drita – maybe once in a .... moon.

11 When I walked into the changing-room, Urša was going through your sports bag looking for money. I caught her .... handed.

12 My gran loves using the Internet. She's a .... surfer.

13 My uncle's a wonderful gardener. He's got .... fingers.

14 That printer I bought last year is useless now. They've stopped selling the ribbons it needs, so it's become a complete .... elephant. I might as well throw it away.

15 Marcella was tickled .... when the President remembered her name.

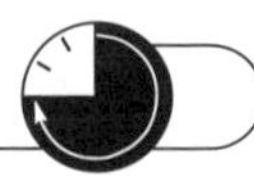

Relationship Questionnaire

Work in pairs. Discuss each question with your partner and choose one of the three options a, b or c. Then see page 63 to find out what kind of boyfriend / girlfriend you are!

1 **It's your birthday. Your boyfriend / girlfriend has promised to take you out to see a film. You get to the cinema on time but they don't show up. When you call them, he / she says they forgot all about the date. What do you do?**

a) laugh it off saying, "It's no big deal. Let's forget about it. Maybe I got the time wrong anyway."

b) explain that you feel let down and ask him / her to try and be more considerate next time

c) slam down the phone and refuse to see him / her again

2 **Your boyfriend / girlfriend says you are eating too many sweets and suggests you should stop eating chocolate. What do you do?**

a) cut out chocolates straight away and start eating salads

b) agree to cut down a little but still eat chocolate when you feel like it

c) tell him / her it's none of their business what you eat, go to the fridge and pig out on your favourite biscuits and cakes

3 **Your boyfriend / girlfriend has picked up some really embarrassing habits from his / her friends, like belching after meals and sniffing loudly while you are talking. What do you do?**

a) smile and say that belching and sniffing and natural things to do

b) bite your tongue in public but take him / her quietly to one side and explain that they should have better manners

c) blow your top and tell him / her that if you wanted to date a monkey you'd go to the zoo

4 **Your boyfriend / girlfriend is always putting you down in front of his / her friends. What do you do?**

a) put on a front and pretend that you don't care, even if it's really getting to you

b) grit your teeth in public but ask him / her to talk it over with you next time you're alone

c) give as good as you get and spill the beans about all his bad habits

5 **Your boyfriend / girlfriend spends money like it's going out of fashion but always claims to be hard up. Now he / she wants to borrow money off you. What do you do?**

a) lend him / her the money happily, no questions asked

b) lend him / her the money but ask them to pay you back before the end of the week

c) turn him / her down and tell them to go and sponge off someone else

6 **What do you do when you're angry with your boyfriend / girlfriend?**

a) bottle up your emotions and say nothing

b) say what you're thinking, get it off your chest and then kiss and make up

c) throw a wobbly, throw things at him / her and then storm out of the room

7 **What do you usually do when your boyfriend / girlfriend introduces you to their friends?**

a) take to them straight away and go out of your way to be friendly

b) hit it off with some of them, but not the others

c) find them a pain in the neck and try to get out of seeing them again

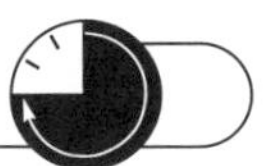

Relationship Questionnaire

8 **What do you usually do when you have an argument with your boyfriend / girlfriend?**

a) give in, throw in the towel and go along with what he / she wants to do

b) try to see both sides of the argument and come up with a compromise

c) stick to your guns, stand your ground and never give an inch

9 **Your boyfriend / girlfriend gives you a present you really hate. What do you do?**

a) tell him / her a white lie and say, "It's wonderful – just what I wanted."

b) come clean and explain why you don't like the gift

c) hit the roof and throw the present back in his / her face

What do your answers say about you?

Mostly As

You are loyal and supportive. You'll stick with someone through thick and thin. But be careful. Sometimes your good nature lets people think they can just walk all over you. Your boyfriend / girlfriend can wrap you round their little finger and get away with murder. Don't let him / her push you around. Sometimes you might need to stand up for yourself a bit more. It's time to stop being a doormat!

Mostly Bs

You're cautious and thoughtful and believe in give and take. You always give your partner the benefit of the doubt but you won't be pushed around. You like to look before you leap and never jump to conclusions. You are cool, calm and collected and prefer to think through the issues involved rather than just blowing your top and losing your rag. Once you trust someone you stick with them through thick and thin. But if someone lets you down, you won't give them a second chance.

Mostly Cs

You are hot-headed and impulsive and fly off the handle much too quickly. Calm down. Try not to lose your rag so quickly. For you, everything has to be cut and dried and there are no grey areas. You always see things in black and white. You won't give people a second chance and you always want to have things your own way. Just remember, good relationships are built on give and take. Try to be more tolerant and understanding.

Match the definitions with the idioms taken from the analyses:

1 to lose your temper
2 to consider all the alternatives before making a decision
3 in all situations, good and bad
4 sharing
5 to characterise everyone and everything as either good or bad, with nothing in between
6 things that are neither completely good nor completely bad
7 to treat someone badly, as if they mean very little to you
8 to defend your rights as a person
9 to have a strong influence on someone so that they do whatever you want
10 to behave badly but not be blamed
11 controlled, rational and sensible
12 to assume that someone has the best intentions, even though you can't be sure that is the case

a) to stand up for yourself
b) grey areas
c) to give someone the benefit of the doubt
d) cool, calm and collected
e) to see things in black and white
f) through thick and thin
g) to wrap someone round your little finger
h) to blow your top
i) to look before you leap
j) give and take
k) to walk all over someone
l) to get away with murder

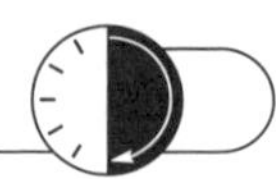

Mind Matching 2

Instructions for the teacher

1. Photocopy the chart below so that there is one for each person in the class.
2. Divide the class into two teams. Each team should nominate someone from their group to be the 'player'. The two players must go to the front of the class, so that they are facing their teams.
3. Give one of the photocopied charts to everyone, including the two players at the front of the class. Ask everyone to complete the first three squares on their chart. The students must not talk to each other or show anyone what they have written.
4. When everyone has finished writing, read out the first question. The two players should then read out their answers to the first question.
5. Everyone from both teams must then read out their answer to the first question. Teams score one point for each person who has the same answer as their team player. (To prevent cheating, move around the class and check what the students have written on their charts.)
6. Read out the second question and repeat the process. When you have heard all of the answers for the first three questions, ask the students to write down their answers to the next three, and continue the game. The team with the most points wins.

Alternative

For a smaller class, play as one team, with one player. Each person scores one point for every answer that matches the player's answer. The winner is the student with the most points at the end of the game.

Write down…

1 ...an item of clothing that you <u>do up</u>.	**2** ...something that might take time to <u>get over</u>.	**3** ...something you have to do when you <u>look after</u> a baby.
4 ...a reason to <u>call off</u> a wedding.	**5** ...two famous people who don't <u>hit it off</u>.	**6** ...a type of food you should <u>keep off</u> if you're on a diet.
7 ...something that <u>drives you up the wall</u>.	**8** ...something that <u>sells like hot cakes</u>.	**9** ...a part of your body in which you can get <u>pins and needles</u>.
10 ...someone who is <u>rolling in money</u>.	**11** ...something you can't do <u>for love or money</u>.	**12** ...something that's as easy as <u>falling off a log</u>.

Around the House

Look at the picture. Find the objects that you need to complete the following idioms.

1 If you have a dark secret, you have a skeleton in your ....

2 A chain smoker smokes like a ....

3 If you waste your money you are pouring it down the ....

4 If you admit defeat you throw in the ....

5 If you pack more than you need when you go on holiday, you take everything but the kitchen ....

6 If you can't decide who to agree with, you sit on the........................... .

7 If someone annoys you, they drive you up the ....

8 If you don't want to face your problems you try to sweep them under the ....

9 When the cost of something rises very quickly, the price goes through the ....

10 If I make you leave the room I show you the ....

11 If you're really busy, you have a lot on your ....

12 If you have to change you plans completely, they go out the ....

13 If someone isn't honest with you, they're leading you up the garden ....

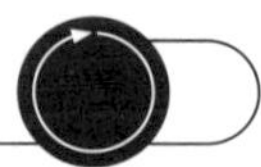

The War of The Roses

Student A

You have six parts of a 12-part story. Your partner has the other six parts. Use the words below to complete your six parts. Your partner will do the same for theirs. Then work out the sequence of the story together.

The words you need to fill in the gaps are:

out (x3) • round • down (x2) • in (x3) • up (x2) • through • on • off • away • into

bone • bush • dawn • paddle pin • legs • heels

A

Mr Swallow curled his upper lip and snarled, "I'm not married and I have no friends so I have no use for flowers. Look at the map, Mr Carter. You have three centimetres of my land. As I told you before, you have until Monday to sort it out. We have nothing else to discuss. Good morning." And with that he slammed the door in my face. 'Charming', I thought. 'How nice.' So, what could I do? I was up a creek without a 1 .... There was nothing else for it. I had to back 2 .... and give 3 .... to his threats. I went home and called the builders and on Monday morning, at crack of 4 .... , they started taking down the fence. As the builders worked, Mr Swallow walked up and down the edge of his garden, map in hand, shouting, "I'm watching you, I'm watching you!", pacing up and down frantically measuring everything that wasn't moving. ☐

B

Mr O'Falltrades nodded. "Double time, new shovels, new spades and a new wheelbarrow..." he said. "Yes, I think I can live with that. Throw in some cream for the bump on my head and you've got a deal." "Double time," Mr Swallow said, "new shovels, new spades, a new wheelbarrow and some cream to put on the bump on your head. Er, right. OK. Fine. And when the doctor turns up. I'll pay the bill. Anything, just as long as you don't take me to court." So a deal was struck and that was the end of it, the end of 'The Wars of The Roses'.

Mr Swallow and I get on much better now. In fact when I saw him in his garden today pottering about in his blue dressing-gown and yellow slippers, he waved at me and walked up to his side of the fence. "Mr Carter?" he said. "I was wondering if I could take 5 .... your offer of the free flowers?" ☐

C

The next morning, I went 6 .... to see him. As I was walking up his front path the lace curtains in his sitting room twitched and I felt as if someone was spying 7 .... me. I knocked on the door. No reply. I knocked again. No reply. "Mr Carter?" I called 8 .... , "Can I speak to you for a moment?" No reply. Complete silence. You could have heard a 9 .... drop. Then the front door opened very slowly, with a high-pitched creaking sound, and there was Mr Swallow in his blue dressing-gown and yellow slippers, with the map of the two gardens in his left hand. "What is it?" he snarled. "What do you want?" "Look," I said. "This is ridiculous. Can I come in and ..." "No, you can't!" Mr Carter replied. "You can't come in. But we can talk here if you like." ☐

D

Last Thursday, a terrible storm blew 10 .... the fence in my back garden. The fence was really old, it was on its last 11 .... , so I wasn't all that surprised that it fell down. But what really annoyed me

was the fact that the fence fell on top of my rose bushes and knocked them flat. I had to throw them all 12 .... What a waste! Now, I love roses, and these bushes were my pride and joy, and for the next two or three days I went 13 .... all sorts of emotions – anger, frustration, sadness, the lot. I was really cut 14 .... about it. But after the initial shock had worn 15 .... , I decided that I'd start all over again, with some new rose bushes and a new and much stronger fence. ☐

❁ E ❁

When the first section of the fence had been moved three centimetres to the left, Mr Swallow took out his tape measure, tied it to the wall of his shed, stretched the tape across the lawn and then held it against the fence. "Four metres!" he shouted. "Four metres exactly. It's mine again. All mine!" But at that exact moment, one of the builders, Jack O'Falltrades, was coming into the garden with a couple of shovels. He didn't see the tape measure stretched tightly across the lawn, twenty centimetres above the grass, and suddenly he was falling, head over 16 .... , and the two shovels were spinning through the air like giant Catherine wheels. There was a thump (as Mr O'Falltrades hit the fence), a couple of thuds (as the shovels hit the shed), a brief silence (as the other gardeners tried to take 17 .... what had happened) and then a strange low cackling sound as Mr Swallow burst 18 .... laughing. But it wasn't funny for Mr O'Falltrades because the impact had knocked him 19 .... He lay slumped against the fence, out cold. ☐

❁ F ❁

Anyway, there he was, on my doorstep, talking at me rather than with me. "May I come in Mr Carter?" he said "I have a 20 .... to pick with you." I was a bit taken aback by his rudeness but I invited him 21 .... and showed him 22 .... the sitting room. "Can I get you something to drink?" I said. "Tea, coffee, a soft drink perhaps?" "No, thank you," Mr Swallow sniffed. "This is not a social call. Now, Mr Carter, I'll come straight to the point. I won't beat about the 23 .... I came home from work just now to discover that you'd stolen my land." "What do you mean?" I said. "I don't understand." ☐

The War of The Roses

Student B

You have six parts of a 12-part story. Your partner has the other six parts. Use the words below to complete your six parts. Your partner will do the same for theirs. Then work out the sequence of the story together.

The words you need to fill in the gaps are:

of • on • back • round • out (x3)
up (x3) • over • off • at • down

pregnant • cheese • knife • hair • fish
eye • rosy • leg • rain

❁ G ❁

"Well," Mr Swallow went on, "the builders have put your new fence up in the wrong place. Here, look at this map. The old fence was four metres away from my tool shed. But the new fence is only three metres and 97 centimetres from my tool shed. In other words, Mr Carter, you've stolen three centimetres of my land. I'm afraid the fence will have to come down. I want my land 1 ...." "Three centimetres?" I said. "You're arguing over three centimetres?" "You bet I am!" Mr Swallow said, "and if you don't sort it out by Monday morning you'll be hearing from my solicitor." And with that he picked 2 .... his map, sniffed and stormed 3 .... of the house. ☐

❁ H ❁

I went down to the garden centre to get some new saplings and I got the builders to put up a new fence to protect them from the wind. So far, so good. But, things didn't quite turn 4 .... the way I'd planned. A few hours after the builders had gone home there was a loud banging at my front door. "OK, OK!" I shouted. "Keep your 5 .... on! I'm coming!" When I opened the door, Mr Swallow, my next door neighbour, was standing there, his face flushed with rage. I've never got 6 .... with Mr Swallow. He's a strange man, a really cold 7 .... I don't know what to make 8 .... him and let's just say that we don't see eye to 9 .... We're as different as chalk and 10 .... ☐

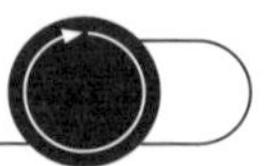

The War of The Roses

I

Mr Swallow was still laughing as I took out my mobile phone and called the hospital. "The doctor's on her way," I said as I switched off my phone. "Oh, and Mr Swallow, I told the doctor to send the bill to you. After all, it was your tape measure that Mr O'Falltrades tripped 11 ...." "But he was moving your fence, Mr Carter. I'm not to blame." "Ah!" I said as I bent down to loosen Mr O'Falltrades' tie. "But my fence was on your land. Look 12 .... the map. It's a good three centimetres your side of the line. I expect you'll be hearing from Mr. O'Falltrades' solicitor in the morning." Mr Swallow changed colour. "Hmmm ..." he muttered. "Good point, Mr Carter. I don't want to go to court ..." And with that, he ran to his shed, took out a bucket, filled it with water, ran back and threw the water over Mr O'Falltrades' face. As Mr O'Falltrades came 13 .... he let out a low, moaning "Ahhh!", shaking his head and spluttering. ☐

J

So the two of us stood on Mr Swallow's doorstep and had a strange and awkward conversation. There were lots of 14 .... pauses and you could have cut the atmosphere with a 15 .... "How about a compromise?" I said after what seemed like hours. "Why don't we leave the fence where it is? It would cost me an arm and a 16 .... to get the builders to move it again. And to make 17 .... for the fact that I've got three centimetres of your land, you can have as many roses as you like from my garden. Just think about it. Just think of all the money you could save. When you want to brighten up your house, or when you friends have birthdays, you won't have to go to the florist's and splash 18 .... on expensive roses, I'll give them to you for free." ☐

K

"Of course," I replied. "What would you like ... flowers for the hall, for the kitchen ...?" "Actually, flowers for a lady," he said, blushing and looking 19 .... at his shoes. "You know the doctor, the lady who came to see Mr O'Falltrades, well, she wanted to write me out a bill and so I invited her into the house, thinking

she could use the kitchen table, and she saw my collection of model trains, (it's my hobby, you see) and it turns out that, by some strange coincidence, it's her hobby too, and we chatted and, well, I ended up asking her out and she's coming round in an hour to pick me 20 .... and we're going to a model exhibition in the Town Hall and ..." "So things are looking up, Mr Swallow?" I said as he blushed an ever deeper shade of red. "Yes, Mr Carter, things are really looking up. It's strange, isn't it, how things turn out. A week ago, it was all rather a mess, wasn't it? But today ... today things are perfect, and I suppose you could almost say that everything in the garden's 21 ...." ☐

L

"There you are," Mr Swallow said, turning to the other builders. "Jack's fine now. Look at him. He's as right as 22 .... , never been better. In fact, that little nap probably did him the power of good. There he is, fit as a fiddle, as good as new, as ..." Mr Swallow broke 23 .... as the five builders formed a circle around him. They didn't look all that pleased. "OK, boys," Mr Swallow stammered. "Take it easy, no harm done, eh? Let's just talk about this ..." "We're listening," one of the builders said. "What did you have in mind?" "Well, erm, why don't we forget about the fence?" Mr Swallow began. "It might as well stay where it is ... after all, what's three centimetres between friends? And let me pay you for today, lads, and ..." The builders moved closer. "On second thoughts, why don't I pay you double time for today?" Mr Swallow went on, his voice a little higher than before. "Double time and some new shovels or spades or whatever you want." ☐

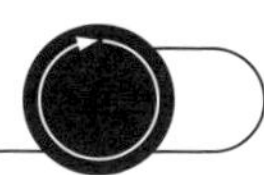

The War of The Roses

Phrasal verbs and idiom quiz

Match the phrasal verbs on the left (1-13) with their definitions on the right (a-m). Do the same with the idioms (14-26) and their definitions (n-z). When you've matched the numbers on the left with the letters on the right, use it as a code to work out the joke at the bottom of the page.

Phrasal Verbs

- ☐ **1** Mr Swallow stormed out of the room.
- ☐ **2** It cut me up when I lost my rose bushes in the storm.
- ☐ **3** Mr Swallow took up my offer of free flowers.
- ☐ **4** Mr O'Falltrades tripped over the tape measure.
- ☐ **5** I went round to Mr Swallow's house.
- ☐ **6** We fell out over the fence.
- ☐ **7** I gave him free flowers to make up for the fact that my fence was on his land.
- ☐ **8** I went through all sorts of emotions when the fence fell on the roses.
- ☐ **9** It took a few moments for the builders to take in what had happened.
- ☐ **10** Mr O'Falltrades came round when Mr Swallow threw a bucket of water over him.
- ☐ **11** There was no need to splash out on expensive flowers.
- ☐ **12** I was up a creek without a paddle so I gave in.
- ☐ **13** We sorted our problem out.

a) to compensate for
b) to stumble and fall
c) to accept
d) to go and visit someone at their home
e) to spend a lot of money
f) to stop being friends
g) to resolve, find a solution to
h) to admit defeat
i) to experience
j) to leave angrily
k) to feel upset
l) to wake up, recover consciousness
m) to realise, understand

Idioms

- ☐ **14** He's a cold fish.
- ☐ **15** Keep your hair on!
- ☐ **16** We don't see eye to eye.
- ☐ **17** I won't beat about the bush.
- ☐ **18** a pregnant pause
- ☐ **19** You could have cut the atmosphere with a knife.
- ☐ **20** It cost me an arm and a leg.
- ☐ **21** He's as right as rain.
- ☐ **22** It was on its last legs.
- ☐ **23** You could have heard a pin drop.
- ☐ **24** I've got a bone to pick with you.
- ☐ **25** at the crack of dawn
- ☐ **26** I was up a creek without a paddle.

n) There was a lot of tension in the air.
o) It was very old.
p) It was very expensive.
q) We don't agree.
r) Calm down!
s) There was no noise.
t) He doesn't show any emotion.
u) I'll get straight to the point.
v) It was hopeless, I couldn't win.
w) Very early in the morning.
x) An embarrassing silence.
y) I'm angry with you because...
z) He's fine.

The Joke

A woman goes into a 20-11-14 shop. The shopkeeper smiles and says, "How can I help you?"
....

"I'd like to buy a 25-7-23-20 please," the woman says.
....

"A 25-7-23-20?" says the shopkeeper. "We don't sell 25-7-23-20-23, madam. I can do you a 12-7-9-23-14-11-15
....

or a 13-22-10-5-6-8-23-12 but I can't sell you a 25-7-23-20, this is a 20-11-14 shop."
....

"You're lying to me," the woman says. "Of course you can sell me a 25-7-23-20 You've got one in the 25-8-19-5-22-25."
....

A Pop Star's Diary

Find the 10 words you need to complete the entries in the pop star's diary in the word circle opposite.

10.30 am

Got up earlier than usual. After breakfast, I drove down to the shops and bought a new mobile phone to contact all my famous friends. It's great, it fits into my pocket and it's as light as a 1 ....

1.00 pm

Had lunch at Bratney Square's house. The vegetables were nice but the meat was as tough as old 2 ....

2.00 pm

Went for a walk and saw Mad Donna jogging in the park. She runs ten kilometres a day. She's as fit as a 3 ....

3.00 pm

Drove back home, but ran over a champagne bottle and got a puncture. The front wheel was as flat as a 4 ....

3.30 pm

Saw Kylie Mini at the supermarket. I called to her, but she didn't answer. (Apparently, she's as deaf as a 5 ....)

5.00 pm

Bumped into Robbie Millions at the recording studio. I accidentally spilt my coffee all over the words to his new song. I went as red as a 6 .... But Robbie didn't mind. He said he didn't like the song much anyway. He was a cool as a 7 ....

7.30 pm

Babysat for my friend Victoria Buckingham. Easy as pie. The child was as good as 8 ....

8.00 pm

Watched an awards ceremony on TV. Why wasn't I invited? I felt as sick as a 9 ....

10.30 pm

Went home and got ready to go to the new disco in town. It was as cold as 10............................ outside so I wore my cool new coat.

4.30 am

Got home. I was absolutely exhausted after my hard day. As soon as my head hit the pillow, I was out like a light.

A Pop Star's Diary

Go round the circle taking alternative letters to find the words you need.

F B E E A E T T H R E O R O B T O C O U T C S U F M I B D E D R L G E O P L A D N P C A A R K R E O P T O I S C T E □

START HERE

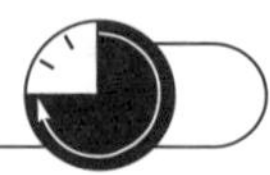

Board Game 3

Instructions for the teacher
Divide the class into groups of four.
Each group will need:
- one copy of the board on pages 74 & 75
- one set of idiom cards
- one set of phrasal verb cards
- a die
- a counter for each player

Rules of the game
Player 1 must role the die and move his / her counter the corresponding number of spaces along the board. If the space that they land on has instructions, such as 'Go forward 3' they must do as the instructions say. If they land on a square that says 'phrasal verbs' or 'idioms', another player must pick up a card from the appropriate pile and read out the question on it. If player 1 gives the correct answer, they may role the die again and have another go. If player 1 gives the wrong answer, play passes to the next person. The winner is the first person to get around the board, from beginning to end.

Idioms

If I'm angry with you about something, what might I say?
a) I've got a bone to pick with you
b) I've got blue blood
c) I'm going to twist your arm
Answer: I've got a bone to pick with you

If you reveal a secret, what do you do?
a) throw the baby out with the bath water
b) put the cat among the pigeons
c) let the cat out of the bag
Answer: let the cat out of the bag

If you're working all day and partying all night, what are you doing?
a) burning your bridges
b) burning the candle at both ends
c) cooking up a storm
Answer: burning the candle at both ends

You're really busy. You've got so much work that you don't know where to start. What kind of animal are you like?
a) a white elephant
b) a headless chicken
c) a church mouse
Answer: a headless chicken

Something is very close to where you live. How do you describe where it is?
a) It's up the garden path
b) It's in my cupboard
c) It's on my doorstep
Answer: It's on my doorstep

If you make an embarrassing mistake, what are you left with?
a) egg on your face
b) water under the bridge
c) a thick skin
Answer: egg on your face

If I tell you off, what do I give you?
a) the benefit of the doubt
b) a piece of my mind
c) peace of mind
Answer: a piece of my mind

You don't have much money – in fact you barely have enough for food and drink. How are you living?
a) ear to ear
b) head to toes
c) hand to mouth
Answer: hand to mouth

You decide to change your bad habits. What do you do?
a) come up trumps
b) come up smelling of roses
c) turn over a new leaf
Answer: turn over a new leaf

Your parents' car is very old. It only just works. What would you say about it?
a) It's got two left feet
b) It's on its last legs
c) It's wrong footed
Answer: It's on its last legs

You're a deep sleeper. What do you sleep like?
a) a log
b) a bird
c) a chimney
Answer: a log

Alessandra's always exaggerating. What should you take everything she says with?
a) a cup of tea
b) a pinch of salt
c) two short planks
Answer: a pinch of salt

I'm studying really hard for these exams. What am I doing?
a) I'm working my socks off
b) I'm keeping my hair on
c) I'm getting shirty
Answer: I'm working my socks off

When you think that somebody is doing something dishonest.
a) you smell a rat
b) you break the camel's back
c) you cry wolf
Answer: You smell a rat

Someone tries to persuade you to do something you don't want to do. There's no way you're going to do it. What are you doing?
a) sticking your nose in
b) sticking to your guns
c) getting the wrong end of the stick
Answer: sticking to your guns

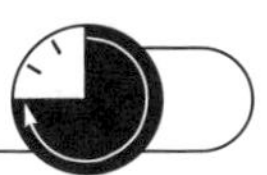

Board Game 3

Phrasal Verbs

Your friend had a cold last week and now you're feeling ill. What must have happened?
a) You passed on the cold
b) You picked up the cold
c) You got over the cold

Answer: You picked up the cold

Henri stopped going to school before he was old enough to do his exams. What did he do?
a) He dropped out
b) He dropped in
c) He passed out

Answer: He dropped out

You meet someone for the first time and both get on really well. What does it mean?
a) You hit it off
b) You hit upon it
c) You hit out

Answer: You hit it off

If something depresses you, what does it do?
a) It gets you down
b) It sets you up
c) It pulls you over

Answer: It gets you down

Some men go into are bank with a gun and make the cashier hand over all the money. What are they doing?
a) They're breaking the bank open
b) They're bringing down the bank
c) They're holding up the bank

Answer: They're holding up the bank

When you put the phone down, what do you do?
a) hang up
b) hang on
c) hang around

Answer: hang up

You have an injection and it really hurts, but after a few minutes the pain goes way. What happens?
a) It puts off
b) It wears off
c) It takes off

Answer: It wears off

If you get fatter, what do you do?
a) You put by weight
b) You put on weight
c) You take on weight

Answer: You put on weight

Simona admitted that she stole the teacher's purse. What did she do?
a) She owned up
b) She made up
c) She took over

Answer: She owned up

When you complete a form, what do you do?
a) You fill it up
b) You fill it in
c) You take it in

Answer: You fill it in

Which sentence is correct?
a) A caterpillar turns over a butterfly
b) A caterpillar turns upon a butterfly
c) A caterpillar turns into a butterfly

Answer: A caterpillar turns into a butterfly

You are in trouble at school, but your best friend defends you. What does he / she do?
a) stands by you
b) stands up to you
c) stands you up

Answer: He / she stands by you

It rained all morning, but now the rain has stopped and the sun has come out. What has happened to the weather?
a) It's cleared off
b) It's cleared up
c) It's cleared away

Answer: It's cleared up

Paul didn't revise for the exam, so pretended to be ill and stayed at home. He wasn't really ill. What was he doing?
a) He was pulling it on
b) He was pulling it along
c) He was putting it on

Answer: He was putting it on

It's late and night and you're tired. It's time to go to bed. What do you do?
a) turn in
b) turn over
c) turn around

Answer: turn in

This will drive you round the bend. Go back 1.	Idiom	Phrasal Verb		Idiom
Idiom				
Life's full of ups and downs. Go back 7.				
Phrasal Verb		**Idioms**		
Idiom				
It's all gone pear-shaped. Go back 4				
Idiom				
Don't cut corners. Go back 2.	Idiom		Phrasal Verb	Idiom

You're on a roll. Go forward 2.

Phrasal Verb

Idiom

You've turned the corner. Move forward 2.

Idiom

Idiom

Phrasal Verbs

Phrasal Verb

Idiom

FINISH

START

This will drive you round the bend. Go back 1.

Phrasal Verb

Idiom

You're in luck. Go forward 3.

Answers

Page 4
Christmas List
Yes: 1, 3, 7; **No:** 2, 4, 5, 6, 8, 9, 10, 11.
The message is: "Wake up Santa."

Page 5
Doctor, Doctor
1. lie down (d), **2.** stick out, work out (b), **3.** turn up (h), **4.** lift up (c), **5.** go out, give up (a), **6.** come back (e), **7.** going on (g), **8.** add up (f), **9.** come across (i).

Page 6
The Elephant Joke
1. into, **2.** down, **3.** up, **4.** by, **5.** out, **6.** back, **7.** onto, **8.** across.

Page 7
Picture Connections
1A + 4B = 6C seahorse; 2A + 8B = 4C fish fingers; 3A + 3B = 1C snowman; 4A + 1B = 5C ladybird, 5A + 6B = 9C jacket potato; 6A + 2B = 7C frogman; 7A + 9B = 2C butterfly; 8A + 5B = 8C lighthouse; 9A + 7B = 3C egg cup.

Page 8
Who's Who?
1.1c, 2h, 3f, 4e, 5b, 6j, 7g, 8a, 9i, 10k, 11d.
2. a) Karen, b) Victoria, c) Henry, d) Trevor, e) Albert, f) Olga, g) Mark, h) Patricia, i) Mr Johnson, j) Jane, k) Greg.

Page 10 & 11
All at Sea
Gap-fill
Student A 1. picture, **2.** cup of tea, **3.** bell, **4.** sail, **5.** feet.
Student B 1. eye, **2.** ropes, **3.** dogs, **4.** shoes, **5.** fish.

The differences
1. In A, there is a picture of a ship hanging up; in B there is a picture of a woman.
2. In A, the sailor is drinking a cup of tea; in B the cup of tea has been knocked over.
3. In A, there is a new bell; in B, there is an old bell.
4. In A, the sail is up; in B, the sail is down.
5. In A, the sailor has got bare feet; in B, he is wearing sandals.
6. In A, you can see both of the sailor's eyes; in B, he is wearing an eye patch.
7. In A, the ropes are piled neatly; in B, they are messy.
8. In A, there are two dogs; in B, there is one dog.
9. In A, there are some trainers; in B there are some boots.
10. In A, the fish are on the boat; in B, they are in the net.

Page 12
Signs
Gap-fill 1. switch off, **2.** give up, **3.** keep off, **4.** slow down, **5.** pick up, **6.** take away, **7.** try on, **8.** check in, **9.** check out, **10.** closing down.
Places 1b, 2d, 3j, 4f, 5g, 6a, 7c, 8e, 9h, 10i.

Page 13
Surfing the web

W	E	P	A	S	S	W	O	R	D
H	F	L	L	W	H	R	O	Z	M
C	Z	U	C	I	U	J	U	F	P
L	O	G	F	T	T	Y	P	E	K
I	P	Y	S	C	R	O	L	L	F
C	B	D	L	H	V	A	Z	D	W
K	P	R	I	N	T	O	R	P	E

Sentences in the correct order
1. (i) Plug the computer in.
2. (c) Switch the computer on.
3. (e) Log on, using your password.
4. (g) Click on the Internet symbol.
5. (a) Type in the website address.
6. (d) Scroll down the page.
7. (f) Print out the information you want.
8. (b) Log off, shut down the computer and switch it off.

Page 14
Carla goes on Holiday
Photocopy the page, stick it on card and cut out the small playing pieces.

Page 18
Fruit Salad
1. pen, **2.** board, **3.** post, **4.** house, **5.** break, **6.** table, **7.** can, **8.** bank, **9.** guide, **10.** jacket, **11.** alarm, **12.** jam.

Answers

Page 19
Sports Quiz
1. off, **2.** up, **3.** out, **4.** in, **5.** up, **6.** out, **7.** out, **8.** off, **9.** out, **10.** up, **11.** on, **12.** on, **13.** up, **14.** off.

Pages 22 & 23
Picture Interviews
Student A 1b, 2b, 3a, 4a, 5a, 6a.
Student B 1b, 2a, 3b, 4a, 5a, 6a.

Pages 24 & 25
The Ladder
1 across: chew; 1 down: clue; 2 down: ways; 3 across: ends; 3 down: eyes; 4 down: sour; 5 across: stir; 5 down: spur; 6 down: rope; 7 across: ride; 7 down: rich; 8 down: ears; 9 across: hits; 9 down: head; 10 down: sack; 11 across: dark; 11 down: deep; 12 down: kill; 13 across: pull.

Pages 28 & 29
Hotel Magnifico
Mona Lott's letter 1. through, **2.** up, **3.** after, **4.** down, **5.** over, **6.** into, **7.** away, **8.** out of.

John Rich's letter 1. down, **2.** through, **3.** up, **4.** over, **5.** into, **6.** away, **7.** out of.

Definitions 1g, 2c, 3e, 4b, 5a, 6f, 7d, 8h.

Pages 30 & 31
Ask a Silly Question
1) 1f, 2d, 3g, 4h, 5b, 6c, 7a, 8e.
3) 1f, 2h, 3b, 4c, 5g, 6d, 7e, 8a.

Page 32
Get Matching
Matches 1d, 2g, 3c, 4a, 5e, 6b, 7f.
Gap-fill a) at, b) over, c) out of, d) up, e) round to, f) away, g) down.

Page 33
The Health Maze
Teabags can cure sore, red eyes.

Pages 36 & 37
What's the Difference?
Student A's differences
1. (spoon) In A, there are three small spoons on the table; in B there is one big spoon.
2. (plate) In A, the plates have flowers on them; in B the plates have stripes on them.
3. (fork) In A, there is an old fork; in B there is a new fork.
4. (feather) There is a parrot on a perch in both pictures. In A, the feather is falling from the parrot; in B the feather is on the floor.
5. (apple) Both A and B have an apple on a plate. In A the apple is whole; in B only the core is left.
6. (bird) In A, the parrot is fat, in B it is thin.
7. (sheep) In A, the sheep is woolly; In B the sheep has been sheared.
8. (tree) In A, there are apples on the tree; in B there are no apples on the tree.

Student B's differences
1. (duck) In A there are two adult ducks; in B a mother duck swimming in front of five ducklings.
2. (haystack) In A, there is nothing on the haystack; in B there is a farm worker with a pitchfork standing on top of it.
3. (chickens) In A there is a chicken looking around the door, in B there is a chicken sitting on her eggs in the corner of the room.
4. (candle) In A, the candle hasn't been lit; in B it has burned nearly all the way down.
5. (smoke) In A the smoke rises from the chimney vertically; in B it rises in a wavy line.
6. (grass) In A the grass is wild and long; in B it has been mown.
7. (book) In A, the book is a cookery book; in B it is a children's book.
8. (bridge) In A, there is a woman crossing the bridge; in B there is a car crossing it.

Page 38
What's the Punch-line?
1. **Definitions** 1d, 2a, 3c, 4b, 5f, 6g, 7e.
2. **Punch-lines** 1d, 2c, 3f, 4e, 5a, 6b.

Page 39
Body Language
1) 1a, 2b, 3b, 4a, 5b, 6b, 7b, 8a.
2) 1h, 2a, 3f, 4c, 5b, 6d, 7g, 8e.

Answers

Page 42
Animal Behaviour
1. bull, **2.** bat, **3.** cat and dog, **4.** snake, **5.** bear, **6.** crocodile, **7.** pig, **8.** snail, **9.** donkey, **10.** wolf.

Page 43
Dinner Time
1. cake, **2.** tea, **3.** potato, **4.** bananas, **5.** butter, **6.** cucumber, **7.** bread, **8.** fish, **9.** peanuts, **10.** grapes. The item that is not used is the bottle of milk.

Page 44
Fact or Fiction?
Snake – anaconda; fruit – banana; country – Canada.

Page 45
Criminal Quiz
1. a – weaker; **2.** k – not punished; **3.** b – more effort; **4.** c – my cousin; **5.** d – no; **6.** j – no; **7.** h – no; **8.** f – no; **9.** e – no; **10.** g – yes; **11.** i – no.

Pages 46 & 47
True Stories
1. true, **2.** true, **3.** false, **4.** true, **5.** true, **6.** true, **7.** true, **8.** true, **9.** false, **10.** true, **11.** true, **12.** true, **13.** false.

Pages 48 & 49
The Perfect Job
Irma is a flight attendant.

Pages 50 & 51
Super Grid: up
1. clear, **2.** save, **3.** build, **4.** tidy, **5.** stay, **6.** grow, **7.** speak, **8.** eat, **9.** cheer, **10.** use, **11.** wash, **12.** put, **13.** look, **14.** give, **15.** do, **16.** break.

Pages 52, 53 & 54
Super Grid: down
1. slow, **2.** put, **3.** get, **4.** calm, **5.** bring, **6.** lie, **7.** go, **8.** run, **9.** wind, **10.** knock, **11.** turn, **12.** live, **13.** let, **14.** hang.

Page 55
Idiom Crossword

Pages 56 & 57
Clowns International
Definitions 1d, 2g, 3f, 4e, 5h, 6k, 7i, 8l, 9b, 10a, 11c.
Gap-fill 1. set up, **2.** set out, **3.** going on, **4.** cropping up, **5.** putting on, **6.** hit upon, **7.** sign up, **8.** find out, **9.** give up, **10.** carrying out, **11.** putting on.

Pages 58 & 59
Pocahontas
Gap-fill 1. set, **2.** named, **3.** set, **4.** burnt/burned, **5.** give, **6.** put, **7.** set, **8.** set, **9.** set, **10.** sets, **11.** try, **12.** pick, **13.** set, **14.** broke, **15.** cut, **16.** come, **17.** made.

Page 60
Missing prepositions a) in, b) out, c) off, d) down, e) up, f) on, g) off, h) across, i) after.
Correct order 1g, 2i, 3d, 4h, 5f, 6e, 7b, 8a, 9c.

Page 61
Colour Codes
1. blue, **2.** red, **3.** blue, **4.** grey, **5.** white, **6.** green, **7.** red, **8.** blue, **9.** black, **10.** blue, **11.** red, **12.** silver, **13.** green, **14.** white, **15.** pink.

Pages 62 & 63
Relationship Questionnaire
1h, 2i, 3f, 4j, 5e, 6b, 7k, 8a, 9g, 10l, 11d, 12c.

Page 65
Around the House
1. cupboard, **2.** chimney, **3.** drain, **4.** towel, **5.** sink, **6.** fence, **7.** wall, **8.** carpet, **9.** roof, **10.** door, **11.** plate, **12.** window, **13.** path.

Pages 66, 67, 68 & 69
War of the Roses
Gap-fill
Student A
1. paddle, **2.** down, **3.** in, **4.** dawn, **5.** up, **6.** round, **7.** on, **8.** out, **9.** pin, **10.** down, **11.** legs, **12.** away, **13.** through, **14.** up, **15.** off, **16.** heels, **17.** in, **18.** out, **19.** out, **20.** bone, **21.** in, **22.** into, **23.** bush.

Student B
1. back, **2.** up, **3.** out, **4.** out, **5.** hair, **6.** on, **7.** fish, **8.** of, **9.** eye, **10.** cheese, **11.** over, **12.** at, **13.** round, **14.** pregnant, **15.** knife, **16.** leg, **17.** up, **18.** out, **19.** down, **20.** up, **21.** rosy, **22.** rain, **23.** off.

Correct order
1d, 2h, 3f, 4g, 5c, 6j, 7a, 8e, 9i, 10l, 11b, 12k.

Phrasal verb and idiom quiz
1j, 2k, 3c, 4b, 5d, 6f, 7a, 8i, 9m, 10l, 11e, 12h, 13g, 14t, 15r, 16q, 17u, 18x, 19n, 20p, 21z, 22o, 23s, 24y, 25w, 26v.

The Joke
A woman goes into a pet shop. The shopkeeper smiles and says, "How can I help you?" "I'd like to buy a wasp please," the woman says. "A wasp?" says the shopkeeper. "We don't sell wasps, madam. I can do you a hamster or a goldfish but I can't sell you a wasp, this is a pet shop." "You're lying to me," the woman says. "Of course you can sell me a wasp. You've got one in the window."

Pages 70 & 71
A Pop Star's Diary
1. feather, **2.** boots, **3.** fiddle, **4.** pancake, **5.** post, **6.** beetroot, **7.** cucumber, **8.** gold, **9.** parrot, **10.** ice.

Material written by: Peter Dainty
Editors: Julie Penn and Cheryl Pelteret
Designer: Christine Cox
Cover Photo: Digitalvision
Cover Design: Kaya-anne Cully
Illustrations by: Steve Lillie

Reprinted in 2008. This edition printed in 2013.

Printed in the UK by Bell and Bain Ltd, Glasgow.